A Medal with Mouse Ears

One Woman's Journey to
Running the Walt Disney World® Marathon

2012 Walt Disney World® Marathon medal © Disney

A Medal with Mouse Ears

One Woman's Journey to
Running the Walt Disney World® Marathon

Mary Townsend

HenschelHAUS Publishing, Inc.
Milwaukee, Wisconsin

Published by
HenschelHAUS Publishing, Inc.
2625 S. Greeley St. Suite 201
Milwaukee, Wisconsin 53207
www.henschelHAUSbooks.com

ISBN: 978159598-529-3
E-ISBN: 978159598-530-9
Library of Congress Control Number: 2017938653

Front cover photo by Mary Townsend

Printed in the United States of America

This book is dedicated to my children,
Stephanie and Joseph;
to my sister, CJ;
and to my best friend and life partner, Stephanie.

Thank you for your unconditional love,
constant motivation, and for always
believing in me and my dreams.
You gave me the courage to try
and shared in my struggles.
You have blessed and enriched my life beyond words.
I love you very much.

… and to Walt Disney,
Entrepreneur and creator of the Walt Disney World
Resort. Thank you for embracing and demonstrating
through your own life that "dreams do come true,
if you have the courage to believe."
These words continue to be my inspiration to dream.

TABLE OF CONTENTS

ACKNOWLEDGMENTS

I would like to express my gratitude to three amazingly strong independent women for their unwavering faith in me and this book: Kimberley Campbell, Deb Karpek, and Kira Henschel.

Their trust, guidance, and support made this publication possible.

Furthermore, I would like to acknowledge with much appreciation Disney Enterprises, who gave me permission to use all required texts and photos to complete this publication.

PROLOGUE

T his is a personal journey of a woman, mother, and career nurse who struggles to find herself physically, emotionally, and spiritually through the challenges, doubts, and sacrifices, in the quest of fulfilling her heart's dream: to finish the 26.2-mile Walt Disney World® Marathon.

As a result of this journey, she is transformed into an independent, courageous woman who discovers her own self-acceptance and spiritual strength, along with the love, happiness, and joy she felt was missing from her life.

This story opens 18 years ago, when the dream of having a "Medal with Mouse Ears" (the Walt Disney World® Marathon finisher medal) first came alive. Fast-forward to a year before the race and the decision to participate.

Each chapter of the quest is recorded with deep soul-searching as she clings to her belief that dreams of the heart do come true, if she only has the courage to believe.

Preface

"Chuang Tzu described the majestic flight of the Peng Bird as the iconic image for great achievements. The mythical bird, with wings spanning many miles, symbolizes the greatness of an individual once he/she commits to his/her mission. The flight of the Peng Bird covers an unimaginably long distance. This refers to the great challenges inherent in a great goal. The journey is long and difficult, and you must reach deeply to summon every bit of strength you have just to stay on course."
– Derek Lin, *The Tao of Joy Every Day: 365 Days, Day 102, loc1499*

Running is a self-love sport. It is a sport where participants hear the whispers of goals that only their hearts know. There are many types of runners. They come in all shapes and sizes, from all walks of life, participating in many different events all over the world. There are the professional runners and the weekend warriors, but all in all, their love for the sport is personal and satisfying.

I present this book with my own vision of running, because I can really only see my sport through my eyes, which run in the middle to the back of the pack. I am not a fast runner; never have been. When I started running at the age of 33, I was more "middle of the pack" than I am at 49. Now I run toward the back and I am okay with that, because I have found my solace and my truth in running, which has taken me many years to reach. I would like to share from my experiences some of the more pertinent general aspects of my love of running and of life as I move into my personal story.

A race distance is the measured distance of that particular event. However, the actual run itself for each participant is very different. The elite runners who line up and start at the front of the pack embark at the sound of the gun, carrying with them the envy of those who are slower and await their own time to start. Their clock time may end hours behind the earlier finishers and that is okay—they just want to run their best, pray to finish, and not be last. T-shirts say it, runners tease each other about it, but finishing last is a very real fear. Realize also that the person running longer is running a harder race. Not everyone is a gazelle gliding along the course; most are not, in fact. They are there for their own dreams and goals and their time is just a byproduct of the cleansing that occurs.

Running a distance event changes its runners; it changes them into better people, stronger, more confident, individuals. Running cleanses the soul of the mental garbage and causes a purging of insecurities and doubts that have festered. Runners who are running a course for hours are pushing themselves to multiple limits, a feat not common in an everyday routine. They are striving to change themselves, heal themselves and find who they know they are through the trials of the distance.

The initial taste of the amazing feeling of self-accomplishment teases the palate of the half-marathoner, who may secretly entertain the thought of someday conquering the feat of running 26.2 marathon miles. The mystique of the marathon captures the soul and breaks it down, removes the unwanted and unneeded pieces, and provides resolve and the path back into a new and empowered being.

"The Wall" that stands waiting around mile 21 is there for the final shattering of the person runners know themselves to be, splintering them completely, breaking them down to their raw core. The rest of the quest, the miles lying ahead, exist to then cleanse the mind, body and spirit of negativity. The final distance then remolds the fractured person into a new being, a whole being—confident, magnificent and complete.

Runners who are struggling, as well as those completing their distance with ease, are all participating for their own personal challenges. Cheer them on. Encourage them. Send them love, light and support. They feel it, they need it, they so appreciate it, and it gives them hope knowing someone, even a complete stranger, believes in them and it helps them validate that they really haven't lost their mind.

Realize that all runners are changing; they are all transforming and they are all facing their fears head on. If you ever have the opportunity, stand at the finish area of a marathon or half-marathon and watch as the runners cross the finish. Witness the miracle, the light of each individual participant shining brightly, as he or she completes the race. Each one transformed into a courageous, more confident athlete, a stronger, more radiant individual, as each runner pushes himself or herself forward to achieve that special dream.

~ Mary Townsend

THE BEGINNING

"A Medal with Mouse Ears." That's how it all started; I had to have one. It was one of those things I had put on my bucket list when I was a much younger runner, thinking I would easily find my way to achieving such a reward. It didn't seem so hard to do. I would train and run and that would be that. However, life has a way of presenting its own plan, and now, 16 years after falling in love with the sport of running, allowing its spirit to integrate into my life, I am preparing to stand at the starting line of a race that may end my running career.

This is my personal story—the struggles, the failures and success, the fears and tribulations, of a mom attempting to balance her life, a marriage, a career, and running, while striving to achieve one of her most coveted dreams.

After the birth of my second child, my son, my life changed, as lives do after the birth of a child, from me finally figuring out the delicate balance of wife, work, and the motherhood of one child. This time, I felt confined and over-stressed. I was working nights, two 12-hour shifts a week at a hospital, and raising my 4-year-old daughter and new baby. The world seemed to be closing in on me. I was sleep deprived, financially we were barely making ends meet, and balancing being a parent with working outside the home nagged at my heart strings and plagued me with constant guilt. My head felt like it was constantly spinning, just like being on a ride and not able to get off; my anxiety was at a premium.

I needed an outlet—one that helped the loud scream I felt on the inside find its way out. I felt I was losing my mind. My sleep patterns were erratic and I could feel the panic and stress swirling within me, building slowly and steadily. I knew I desperately needed a release. I was beginning to feel like I was caged, trapped, unhappy, tired, and alone, with no release, no dreams, no relief.

So, one beautiful day, when the space of time presented itself, and I could stand the pressure cooker no longer, I put on my sneakers, opened the door, and took off running. I can't tell you what or why it felt like the right thing to do; I knew I had to release the energy and anxiety that continued to percolate within.

I didn't walk first, warm up, begin slowly—I *ran*. I felt the ground beneath my feet, the sun on my body, and the fresh spring air was amazingly refreshing against my cheeks. The trees smelled deliciously fragrant. But most of all, I felt free. Yes, free. I could feel myself begin to let go of the bindings and chains I felt had begun to weigh me down. I reveled in the movement of my body, feeling the breath in my lungs, the beating of my heart— and I could feel ME.

Wow, I *was* still alive! Down deep inside, buried by responsibilities, new roles, new job, new anxieties, and new expectations. Beneath the clutter of what I felt had become my life and all the emotional baggage, I was still really alive!

I cried—hard. I ran and I cried, out loud, releasing what needed to be let go at that moment. I could feel the tears filling my eyes, then streaming down my cheeks, clouding my vision and cleansing my heart. It was no longer the outside of me I saw and felt, but the inside of me started to be present. The person I knew I was, or at least, used to be—she was there.

The path before me was blurred by tears and I could no longer see where I was running. Instead, I was led by the girl inside, who was so hurting and waiting to be loved. I kept moving, through the swirl of emotions, letting go, relaxing. I was able to breathe again. Huge, deep breaths. I felt alive again. The strength of my emotions shattered the shell I had built around me, and I felt alive once more.

I ran for 25 minutes without stopping. It felt remarkable. I came home refreshed, tired and changed. For the next couple of days, my legs were quite stiff from my running "fling." Nevertheless, it had been well worth the release. I was filled with gratitude for the intimate moment I had with myself. I smiled through the inability to bend my legs with ease, relieved that I was still alive somewhere amidst the chaos I felt my life had become.

During the week, as the soreness subsided, the stress and anxieties began stirring around me again. This time, I felt panic creeping up like an unwanted guest, a noticeable and ever present incline. My thoughts immediately shifted to running. I desired a release and couldn't wait until I could fit running into my hectic schedule again.

Several days later, when the opportunity presented itself, I laced up my sneakers and bolted out the door. At first, my body was just a little stiff and then—*freedom!* I began running through the anxieties and fears, the obstacles that were robbing me of happiness, and any kind of peace and again, another good cry resulted.

I bawled, letting go of the pain and frustration bottled up inside, releasing all those restrictive feelings to the running gods, who were most happy to remove the burdens from my shoulders. I was grateful and at the end of the run, I was *ME* again.

Arriving at my back door, I was peaceful and tired, thankful for the two beautiful children, who are my everything, whom I've been blessed with, a career I enjoyed, and the family who loved me. After my run, I was able to see my life from a completely different perspective. In that moment, I was appreciative and relaxed. My stressors seemed trivial compared to the blessings I had.

Still breathing hard, I said a quiet prayer of thanks for the gift of being able to see my life without the noise and demands of the world, of being able to feel the love that surrounded me. I was able to see the good in my life, to find and become reacquainted with myself, who I had thought had been lost forever.

It was at that moment I knew I was meant to run. Running would provide the balance my life was lacking, the sentry that would stand strong in the face of despair, the partner that would listen to me cry and shout aloud and most of all, the activity that would be my friend.

I had found my new outlet—running. I learned I could share my thoughts and release my fears to the running gods. So, I would like to say that gradually, I became a runner and an athlete, fitting my new-found friend into my busy schedule. I would like to say that ... but in actuality, those sentiments are very far from the truth.

What's true is I loved running. However, my busy schedule and lack of sleep dictated something different. I was tired most of the time; the balancing act that had become my life was constantly gyrating off center and I could not get a good grip on it.

I had two small children, a marriage that was not going as originally planned, and the relentless night work motivated the desire for sleep in place of activity. I napped when my kids napped, and when my daughter didn't nap anymore, I made arrangements for her to stay with a neighbor who had a licensed daycare in her home, so I could sleep a couple of hours. My daughter protested, and I felt myself burning out. It turned out that as long as I picked her up before lunch and we ate together, we had a deal. Otherwise, no chance!

I continued to adjust my schedule frequently to accommodate my responsibilities as a mom and to take care of the constantly looming financial burdens. At the time, I worked as a "pool nurse," someone who accommodates the hospitals' overflow need for nurses, but doesn't require any commitment other than showing up. I got paid when I worked. That was it. If there wasn't a need the night I was scheduled to work, my shift was cancelled.

The inconsistency of my employment and irregular sleep patterns continued to render me anxious and exhausted. Running rapidly became a memory I only wished I had the energy to do. The memory of the freedom faded as the piles of emotional stress, responsibilities, financial demands, and the lack of self-balance began to build. I felt scared and quite alone among the clutter.

The cold winter months crept in and darkness claimed the lighted evenings. It felt like it was always dark, gray, and cold. The memory of the warm sun on my face and light breeze on my cheeks was a fading one.

I trudged through my days as expected, doing my best to juggle my increasing responsibilities resulting from a failing marriage, and losing myself in the numb motions that had become my married life. This is not to say I didn't love my children. Actually, the opposite rings true. Their love is what drove me to go on, to keep it all together. They remained my focus and my beacon; they were the lifesavers I clung to so tightly that prevented me from drowning in an existence I felt was no longer my own.

My crazy schedule kept shifting and another spring arrived with a move to a larger home to accommodate our family of four.

With the newness in the air and the days steadily growing longer, I felt the stirrings of a new hope deep within.

Change was in the air, and feeling bold with blind faith, I decided to leave the hospital setting and the dreaded 12-hour night shifts. So I ventured bravely into a personally and professionally uncharted area of home-care nursing. I accepted a position and experienced on-the-job training as I learned a completely different side of nursing care. My new role would allow for strictly day work, a flexible schedule, more time at home, and I would be working outside, driving and visiting patients in their homes.

Oh, how I love to be outside! This seemed perfect! Every day, Monday through Friday, I packed up my kids, put my daughter on the school bus and drove my son to daycare. Then I went to see my patients in their homes, hurried back to pick up my son and to arrive home just before the school bus dropped off my daughter. I was scheduled, organized, and in a rigid, but safe, routine.

There was little room for traffic jams, patient emergencies and other unforeseen acts of God. I *HAD* to be home before the school bus, or my daughter would have a complete meltdown right there on the sidewalk. Of course, my neighbor was home in case of an emergency, but to a five-year-old, the only emergency is that Mommy is not home.

This schedule worked. I was able to learn the home-care business and begin to balance my sleep patterns. Even though my son was young, he adjusted well to daycare and even enjoyed going. Initially, the guilt I associated with leaving him weighed me down so much that there were times I felt like I couldn't catch my breath. Slowly, however, that trapped feeling lightened as he adjusted. In addition, I felt more rested and less anxious, which allowed me to be more present in my children's lives.

I was just as busy as any mom with two small children, battling the guilt and insecurities of motherhood with no manual to refer to, and feeling like the learning curve was never-ending. I missed my kids all the while I was working, anxious to hurry home in time. I knew I had to do what was best for all of us. I started to come to the realization that I desperately needed to get a grip on my life, see it for what it was, and I needed to emerge from the gloom that consumed my thoughts and the constant loneliness I felt in my married life. But how?

As spring slipped into summer, and the warmth of the bright, sunny days emerged with blooming trees and green grass, I entertained the thought of running again. The memory of how I felt when I was running was stored in my thoughts and kept securely in my heart. It was there, making many attempts to surface over the past several months, banging against my stubborn head urging me to find the time and set it free.

But, I had kept it still, ignoring the plea, and gathering excuses to keep that sensation of freedom at bay. The self-imposed cage seemed to be working—schedules, responsibilities, finances, anxieties—with my mind winning the internal battle, to dim my inner light, my dreams, and quiet my heart's desires.

Then, one beautifully warm summer Saturday morning, while my family lay sleeping, I succumbed to the noise. I couldn't stand it. I finally listened to the constant, internal desire to get up and move. I laced up my sneakers and headed out the door, timing myself precisely to be home a few minutes before my family was scheduled to wake up.

This would become my routine, my outlet, my own. I would make time to become a runner, and in turn, the time to grow, learn, and discover who I was. It was up to me to make it happen. Running became my moment of freedom, of alone time, of crying, singing, laughing, moving, flowing, and living—using all of my senses, connecting with myself, allowing all emotions to waken and come alive. It became my time to feel the warm sun or cool rain on my face, the sturdiness of the earth and of complete BE-ing in myself.

Years began to pass, and the management of my life's responsibilities found a status quo balance of routine. I continued running and merged my sport and love of it into my daily routine. I loved being a mom and enjoyed playing an active role in my children's lives. My happiness found itself in their lives, watching them grow, explore, and challenge life. Their joy reflected back at me, lightened my one-time heaviness, and a rhythm began to once more settle into my life, carrying us on a continued current of passing years and memories.

Magic

The mystique of the Walt Disney World Resort captures the innocent and recues the lost. What I mean by that is magic and dreams are acceptable and commonplace in Disney, thereby reaching into our souls and tugging at the very core of our inner child existence. As adults, life is stern and at times harsh; as children, all wonder lies before us, just waiting for us to explore.

The magic of the Walt Disney World Resort and its promise that "dreams do come true" I would have to say, I have always believed. The lyrics of the many songs with encouragement of the mouse and all his friends promise this. This phrase personifies the teachings and the strength of the "power of intention." It does, in its purest form, instruct us to listen to our hearts, focus, and go for our dreams.

Walt Disney was a visionary who took risks and wanted to improve the world in which he lived. His example echoes throughout the very existence of the Walt Disney World Resort and flows as a magical undercurrent, inspiring the inner child to come alive, play, dream, and believe.

I am a dreamer and I embrace the power the dreams and intention, of wishes and hopes and knowing that the originator of this magnificent place was also a dreamer and encouraged it in others. The reassurance of the power of intention and the example of Walt Disney's life made me believe I could also possess a potential for living my dreams. It gave me the hope to pursue them, believing that there is restitution, and my dreams were not silly, and I was not crazy, but thoughts, which if intended upon, would become manifestations of my heart's dreams.

Jiminy Cricket, whose character is the physical embodiment of the conscience, encourages everyone during the Wishes Nighttime Spectacular to be courageous, brave, and to believe in themselves and their dreams. The words of a sage couldn't be clearer. If the power of intention is set, focused on with love, along with the power of positive thinking, it will materialize. He guides us to follow the gut feeling, the solar plexus, which controls how one reads and interprets a situation or encounter on the spiritual level. We learn as children to listen to our heart, our gut, and see how the situation "feels." It is the same practice now used as adults when we manifest our reality with intention and love.

This is the core of my belief; I acknowledged it years ago and validate it with my current spiritual practice, however; not actually making the connection between the Walt Disney World Resort and how much I enjoyed being there until I realized how important it was for me to stay true to my heart, wishes, and dreams.

The Walt Disney World Resort was the place, the only place on earth, where I felt as innocent as a child and hopeful for life and happiness. I cannot say I was entirely happy in my life until this time, yet when at the Resort, I was. I was drawn to the ease in which the magic swirled and the encouragement that when things do go bad. I only had to wish and believe.

I so wanted to believe. I wanted to believe the unhappiness I was feeling in my life, especially in my marriage, would just be a passing breeze if I set my sights on my heart with its intentions in motion. I was waiting for the magic to appear and save me. I was looking for fate to light the way out of the sadness and anxiety that had crept into my daily existence.

The encompassing magic promised that if my heart was in my dreams, my dreams would come true. I knew in my heart, this simple, yet genuine, philosophy lived in me and I so wanted to believe the promise set forth. It was if a soft, warm light in me was the magic and I just had to allow it to shine by staying focused and believing.

My inner child believed and she wanted so badly to be happy and carefree. I felt her come alive when I was at the Walt Disney World Resort and even in anticipation of vacationing there, listening to the songs in preparation for our trips. We diligently saved and tried to get there whenever we could; I worked extra days. My kids and I used to sing the songs in the car, each of us having our own parts to sing, sharing the belief that when we arrived at our destination, our lives would be free of the chaos of reality, and our hearts would vacation. I knew my inner child would emerge and have a chance to play. I sang aloud with them and my heart would ache; I would also silently hope and pray that the simplicity of the promise truly existed.

At the time, I didn't know about the power of intention and the ability to navigate the waters of my life. I only knew I was searching for something I was sure just had to be out there, a release of some kind to set my heart free. I felt the freedom when at the Walt Disney World Resort—it was a taste of happiness, cherished and rare.

So, running the Walt Disney World® Marathon was not just an endurance race for me set upon an imaginary list. It was the spiritual combination of my inner child and my adult self, an event that would cleanse and fuse the fractured pieces of a person I had become in so many areas of my life. It wasn't going to be so easy to let the desire to run it, drift off into the ethers of life. Not running due to the obstacles that presented themselves offered no excuse. Running toward a "medal with mouse ears" was the vehicle I believed I needed to usher me toward the person I was meant to be.

This race was my dream. I believed it would blend and balance the purest, most innocent wishes and desires of my heart with the running I had grown to love. It would help me to reach past the stressed, unhappy adult I was and coax my inner child to the surface, have her meet the woman I had become and hopefully, together join hands and finally find peace.

I secretly set my sights on my goal—we could vacation at the Resort during the Walt Disney World® Marathon weekend and enjoy all the runDisney festivities. I made a wish—I would someday enter the marathon—as I stood before the Cinderella Castle, crying, immersed in the guarantee of promises made as the Wishes Nighttime Spectacular fireworks exploded over my head.

A twisted path with unexpected turns led to the manifestation of the Walt Disney World® Marathon in my life. Sometimes I think if anyone had told me I would have to wait eleven years to run, I would not have believed it.

My sister's favorite questions to me are, "When we're 80 and sitting on the porch talking, what would you say to me that you would have wished you did in your life and didn't?" "You know, when you look back, will you have anything left undone that you really wanted to do?" And as always, she would answer her own question with: "I hope your answer is no."

I wouldn't be able to answer "no" without completing this race. I have always thought one of the most coveted rewards would be to run through all the parks—Magic Kingdom, Epcot, Disney's Hollywood Studios, and Disney's Animal Kingdom, and especially the Cinderella Castle. I motivated myself by saying that the Walt Disney World Resort would close the parks just for me to run and enjoy, just to be able to combine my love for running with my love for the magic of the Resort into a one-time experience. The thought constantly echoed within me. I couldn't shake it, so I placed this event on my to-do "bucket list." Once that was completed, I would be able to look my sister in the eye when we are 80 and say no.

The Walt Disney World® Marathon takes place in the month of January, and as soon as the race weekend is completed, the website begins posting information for the following year's event. Well, that was all my kids and I had to hear—the Walt Disney World Resort had its own marathon.

"How cool would that be, Mom, to run through the Walt Disney World Resort?"

Cool indeed! My heart began to yearn for a medal with mouse ears. I sent in my entry and set my sights on my new goal—running in the 2001 Walt Disney World® Marathon. I was pumped and ready to train. I had maintained my practice and love of running. Besides, I was running regularly. I had completed the New York City Marathon and other distance races. I knew what to expect and felt I was ready.

Feeling eager, I entered the Ocean Drive Marathon, which runs from Cape May to Sea Isle the first week of April. I stayed with my weekly 20 to 25 miles and was never fond of stretching, but I felt good about the race. I thought the experience would be a nice reminder and tune up for my pending January event. At least I thought so.

I upped my training mileage a little, dropped back down to my pre-marathon weight and picked up a wonderful running partner, my sister's new boyfriend. He is built like a runner—tall, thin with long legs—partnering with my 5 foot 2 stature. I simply couldn't compete with his stride, however. It was his first marathon and I was "experienced," or so I thought.

We ran together the whole race. My sister started with us, but had signed up for only the first 10 miles, which ended on the sunny and beautiful New Jersey Wildwood Boardwalk. Off the boardwalk, the clouds overtook the sun, the weather changed, and the ocean mist was cold as it blew against my face and made me feel damp all over. We ran onto the streets, over bridges, and only the right side of the street for almost the entire rest of the race.

That visual is important, because by mile 18 or so my left leg started to burn with each step. No, not one of those pains you can run through—it was the kind of pain that only gets worse with time. I ran slowly, then even slower, no PR coming out of this race. My left leg burned like fire with every step, a pain not familiar, yet at the moment forgotten. God forbid, I get swept or come in last. I pushed on through the searing hot pain in my outer left knee and down my leg with stiffness almost immobilizing me.

All kinds of people were passing me. I had to keep moving. My sister's boyfriend stayed with me the entire time, slowing his pace to keep with mine. I finished the race in about 5:35:00, something like that, I could barely walk and once I got to the finish line, I was limping. I was terrified. What if I had just blown out my leg?

The next week I rested, no running, and my leg felt fine. I was relieved. I hadn't really done any damage. Maybe I was a bit embarrassed with my sister's new boyfriend, but I came through and wasn't swept or last. I decided to head out for a short run to keep my legs moving. I laced up and headed out the door for an early, quick mile or two.

With my first two strides, pain like no other screamed up the outer side of my left knee.

What had I done? I could barely move my leg by the time I came home. I couldn't even climb up my steps without excruciating pain. It was supposed to be an easy tune-up race! I was scared, really scared. What had happened? I had just run a marathon only a few months ago and finished healthy—exhausted, but healthy.

After several doctor's appointments, an X-ray, and an MRI, I was told I had Ileotibial Band Syndrome (IBS) and was looking at nine months of therapy, and then finally a cortisone injection before I could even think of running.

To prevent permanent damage and heal, I did as directed through many tears and let go of my upcoming January dream.

Twelve months later, recovered and healthy, I stayed true to running, both for the fitness and the meditation. It was a regular part of my life and it was mine alone. I felt empowered when I ran. I felt strong both physically and emotionally. It was my mediation, my alone time and it brought me solace.

Before I realized it, years passed and I could no longer hear the echoes of my dream and the opportunity of a Walt Disney World® Marathon medal faded. I could no longer visualize my "medal with mouse ears." I read about the Marathon in my magazines and continued to dismiss the desire. I tucked it deep within as to not feel the disappointment that surfaced.

I continued in the regular routine that was my life. Both the financial and personal expectations had dissolved any potential dreams I had of going. I had begun to suffer from chondromalacia in my right knee—"runner's knee." It had gotten so intense, so painful that I underwent laparoscopic surgical repair, so that I could even run again. Without the procedure, my running days were over.

The surgeon informed me my knee was like a car, that I only had a finite amount of miles in it before it would not allow me to run on it. Take care and be prudent, no more long-distance running, easy miles and my knee would last much longer.

Trials

I knew I needed to regularly lace my shoes and run. Run from my life, run from fear and run from the demands that were now darkening me again with expectations I could no longer keep afloat. My marriage was completely falling apart. I needed to run. I needed that hour to pick up the pieces of "me" and face my day.

Things at home took precedence over any intimate personal desires in my heart. I had let go of who I was, in spite of my infrequent runs, and exercising physical prudence and shorter distances. I was completely lost and treading water in a marriage that was drowning me. I could barely breathe. I was choking and finding the inner child. Well, I think she just ran and hid. I was out of balance, and I knew it. I felt it.

My sister had moved to South Carolina for work and visited only a couple times a year. During one visit, she visibly noticed that the light in my eyes had dimmed. She decided to do something about it and surprise me. That year, my sister said it was a Christmas and birthday gift and she booked me to slip away to the Walt Disney World Resort for race weekend, run, and come home. She and her now-husband would meet me there from South Carolina and cheer me on.

So in 2007, I re-entered the Walt Disney World® Marathon and even bought a computer chip to place on my running shoe. I was going for the gusto.

I was set. I was going. I was 45. I had slacked off any intense running due to my repaired right knee and crumbling home environment and therefore my running time came at a premium. I started training slowly and carefully and whenever I could. I wasn't going to let my dream slip again. I was determined to stay focused.

September approached and I once again entered the Philadelphia Distance Run, a half-marathon of 13.1 miles. I ran well that bright, sunny day and felt good. The Walt Disney World® Marathon was right around the corner in January and I was very much looking forward to accomplishing my goal.

My marriage continued to crumble. I was now separated and going through a tumultuous divorce. Life was not pleasant; running time continued to be at a premium and finally my attorney suggested it wouldn't be a wise move to leave my home and children for three days, even if it was for a structured, planned event.

I was devastated, completely crushed. Running was what was keeping my head above water in all of this turmoil. Besides my children, running was all I had that was consistent and reliable. Running was my faithful partner that listened and allowed me to be myself and be free. It had become my solace.

But suddenly, running was no longer an outlet; it was a pawn in a game I wished I wasn't playing. I called my sister and we cancelled the trip, knowing it was the wise thing to do. Nevertheless, once again I was letting go of my dream.

Years would pass again, and the hope and desire to run my dream settled itself into a permanent backseat. Actually, I had let it go and given it up for a wish of the heart that was just that, a wish. Nice to have, but as time passed, more and more unrealistic.

I had also stopped running altogether. My life had taken a self-initiated sharp turn and through the demands that consumed me the year leading to my divorce date, I let running go. I ate out of stress and gained weight. Following the final court's decision, I began to restructure my life, falling out of the routine of running and meditating and striving only to recover my physical environment and re-establish my home.

I now had a new house and a new path and all-but-fractured pieces of me lying on the floor. It seems the running and the mediating would be the sensible route to travel. However, life-changing events, even if self-initiated, fracture the soul. I felt shocked, as if someone or something shattered me into a million little pieces and I couldn't pick them up but one at a time. They were sharp and they hurt and I didn't want to reassemble them into the person I was. So the pieces lay loose, one on top of the other as I waited for the vibration of the shock wave to quiet.

My goal was creating a home, taking care of my children every other week, and making other adjustments that came with starting over. I was restructuring my life, releasing the old and allowing the new. I also now could see a light, a light of newness and possibilities, that warmed my new path, and even with all my changes, less anxiety, and finally hope appeared.

The relief that came from the finality of my decision to divorce released the heaviness that weighed my soul. I could finally take a deep breath and feel it all the way through, not struggling against a weight on my chest and in my heart and the confines of unhappiness.

Hope was alive and I was learning and recovering slowly, but I needed some help sorting through the splinters on the floor. I needed time away to mend the wounds, the hurt, so I committed to a Shamanic retreat in Sedona. To tell the truth, I was out of my comfort zone even planning such a trip, yet I felt the calling to go. I went with an open mind and a broken soul and returned repaired and renewed.

There, my pieces had been delicately rearranged in place, with love, awaiting final adhesion from me through commitment, promise and growth. My separate parts realized, identified, and were given back to me as a gift to open.

Returning home from Sedona, I felt renewed and able to move ahead following my life's chosen path, leaving the hurt behind and finally breathing through my life. I was no longer drowning, no longer choking from unhappiness and anxiety. It was now up to me to mend the pieces in place, fuse the parts of me that had been badly bruised into the person I was meant to be. I had been given the guidelines; it was now up to me to follow the course and grow.

THE COMMITMENT

When I decided to commit to running the Walt Disney World® Marathon, I was also committing to changing my life, to accomplish my dream. I was ready to move ahead and felt strong enough now to face the trials that would envelope me as I healed.

Over a year had passed since my trip to Sedona and I was reexamining my life and the things I had let go. I didn't return to running following my retreat. I couldn't commit to the daily ritual, although I had found myself moving forward, taking only baby steps along my new path.

I ventured into new waters, took on a new job and moved ahead creatively and professionally. I truly was taking baby steps, fearing that one morning I would wake up and find all my happiness and hope were all just a dream, and terrified that I would be back where I was, suffocating in my old married life. I needed time to heal. I needed time to just breathe as almost to not scare myself away from the growth that was occurring. I was slowly, lovingly, mending myself with easier, simpler tasks, and loving life. Spiritually, I began to settle into myself and open up to the person deep inside.

One day, my children—with minds that never forget—challenged me. My daughter, excited to run her first 13.1 Disney Princess Half-Marathon, relentlessly nagged at me and my dream to run the full marathon. Chiming in was my son, who couldn't wait to go to the Walt Disney World Resort again. "How cool would it be to go for race weekend?"

"Yes, it would be cool. However, we're on a tight budget and I haven't run in years." I entertained the thought and then dismissed it. Their coaxing and enthusiasm rekindled my long-suppressed desire for a medal with mouse ears and my son, the baseball player, said he would sign up for his first race, the Walt Disney World Half-Marathon, 13.1 miles, if I ran.

I was much older now, overweight, and I knew the challenges of running marathons and the toll they took on the body. My right knee still hurt from time to time and I was so out of shape. I didn't want to commit to the race; I didn't want to cause an upheaval in the new life I had begun to build. I wasn't sure I was emotionally strong enough to add the commitment to my philosophical plate and rearrange my life once again.

I told myself I was prepared to let it go and face my sister when she asked about my dreams. I had my trusty bag of excuses sitting close to me as to why I didn't complete my dream and yet, as I listed them, none of them held any weight.

Excuses are just that—excuses. There is no substance to them. They are empty words of fear that sabotage the soul and feed the mind with nonsense. I knew this.

Both my children were becoming runners and finding the plethora of emotions incorporated in running. They were grasping the baton, reflecting my example and challenging themselves. Their enthusiasm and determination made me so proud of them; it touched the core of my being and brought tears to my eyes.

My children were sharing my love for the sport, a sport I had stepped away from and one in which they were also maturing. I knew in my heart it was time to commit, time to reach for the same baton and lead the way as I had done before. It was time to venture out of my comfort zone once again. I knew I needed to take the risk to grow. It was time for me to finally follow my heart and go for my dream.

I selected January 2, 2011, as the start date of the "year before my marathon" and visited a local fitness center to investigate my advantages. To my surprise, it was just what I needed. Twenty-four-hour access and a minute from my home, with my main concern being able to run in the winter cold, those dreaded long runs that now awaited me. I signed up and met with a personal trainer, who showed both my daughter and me how to use the equipment, including the scale. I had taken the first step.

At this time of my quest, I decided to be brave and step on the scale—the tall, metal beast—to obtain my dreaded "baseline" weight. I weighed in at 157 pounds, and yes, I am only 5 foot 2. I felt my heart sicken as it sank—I had done even more damage than I had imagined! Knowing this and the instability of my right knee, I took a deep breath and decided that I wasn't going to let anything steal my dream. Not this time! If I focused and visualized, I could accomplish my goal. So I made my plan.

My first challenge was to take off the weight. I had mentally planned a slow, but steady, regime to visit my new home—the fitness center—and develop a relationship with my old friend and challenger—the treadmill, and get walking.

I couldn't even think of running! I hadn't run in years and my body told the tale of comfort food, stress eating, age and neglect. I had long put away my pre-divorce clothes and settled for unfamiliar sizes. I have to say, I missed my waist. I would put on clothes that hid my midline, knowing that under the layers I had acquired, was my waist, somewhere, and my runner's body were hiding.

It was difficult to look at myself in the mirror. I didn't recognize me! I felt as though I had borrowed the body of another and yearned to return it. I knew this new goal was the carrot I needed to find my runner self. She was obviously lost and my physical appearance was just the outward sign that I needed to start looking.

I decided I was mentally ready to hit the gym, watch my diet and work out. My only hope was that my body, which I had mindfully neglected, would cooperate. Now I would like to say I got up early every day and worked out with ease and developed a flow. Not so.

I had not counted on the difficulty I would encounter trying to find time in my day to attend a 24-hour gym! I struggled for the next three weeks to establish a routine. I knew I needed a routine, a regular niche in my day where I retreated to the confessional of the treadmill. I had experience there. Back in my running days, I was able to get up early in the morning, before work, and run. It's what I did every morning. The alarm went off and somehow, I got up and got moving. Then I had anxiety to run off and the desire to quiet my head. My life now had become lighter and more peaceful and the desire to "run away from it" had lifted, leaving me unmotivated and struggling with a new routine.

The next three weeks I wrestled with myself and my schedule, to find the time I needed to make my intention materialize. I knew this was what I wanted to do; now I had to make the room in my already busy schedule, on a regular basis. I knew I had to get my body moving to even begin to lose the weight and build any kind of endurance.

Getting up before work was not an option, not this time around. I felt already too tired to cut into my sleep time. I would make time in the late afternoon, before dinner. It seemed logical. I could take my son to high school, and then go to work. After work, I'd hit the gym before the evening meal. It took so long for my stomach to empty that I would have to wait a minimum of two hours after a meal to be able to perform any activity. So after work seemed like the best time. I planned it and decided to go. I laid out my exercise clothes before I left in the morning, then once home, I changed and headed out the door, so I wouldn't be distracted and find a reason not to go.

I have to say that everyone else at the gym also felt that after work and before dinner was the perfect time, too. The treadmills were at a premium and remember, this is January in New Jersey;

it's cold outside and everyone has also made his or her New Year's resolution to lose weight. I discovered that I had to be at the gym by 4:30pm to be able to get a treadmill without waiting, and so it motivated me even more to get out the door when I arrived home. My best friend and I had a standing appointment to meet at the gym and walk. It was important we get treadmills together, so we made sure we kept to our time.

And so, I walked. It was so hard not to follow the desire of my heart and break into a running stride. I knew how to do it. I had done it for years without a thought, and now all I could do at this moment in my life was walk. I read once that one third of the action of running is spent in the air and once on the treadmill, the longing for the freedom to fly burned inside of me. I knew the limitations I faced with my body, with my knee.

The words, *"You know you only have so many miles in this knee ... "* continued to echo in my head and I was scared. Had I taken on more than I could physically do? What was I thinking? I knew the extra pounds I was carrying would just crush my knee and destroy any chances of reaching my goal, especially if I broke into a stride. I was disappointed in myself that I had let go of the athlete I had been, and buried her under the physical and emotional wreckage of comfort eating and neglect that had consumed her earlier life.

I had to fight the urge to erupt into the runner who was aching to be set free. I was excited! Excited to run, excited to fly as I propelled myself forward. I had to gently tell her that she would be allowed to find her way out in a little while. I had to talk to her and let her know that the body she was used to moving was heavier and slower and a little older and she would have to wait until the time was safe.

She and I battled almost every evening in January, but I walked. I walked and talked with my best friend. We caught each other up on our day's activities and before I knew it, I had a regular routine, one I even looked forward to.

Now January was not just all about finding my way to the gym. It also held the keys to my stress eating and poor diet that had taken over my actions in these past three years. I now had to do a complete about-face and pay attention to what I was actually eating. Oh yes, I have done this before. Easy, right? All I had to do was jump onto the "exercise train" and it would all fall into place.

Not so.

I had become accustomed to the comfort food, the starches that tasted so good and the sweets that calmed me in times of panic and distress. I had the body to show it. My digestion was terrible, my stomach always felt full and bloated and the last thing I could say is that I was "regular." I was never hungry, yet I always wanted to eat. The sense of heaviness I carried made me sluggish, tired, and physically so uncomfortable.

Maybe the weight gain and discomfort were in fact a medical issue, so I decided to have them checked out. Then I could say that I can't run the race and have a real excuse to remove it from my bucket list. So, that's what I did. I had a complete medical work up, blood work, upper GI and emptying scan. I saw my primary doctor and the specialist. I did what they said and continued to keep my commitment to walk. I figured the walking couldn't hurt—it's what people do. I wasn't going to give myself any more excuses, not yet at least.

I walked on the treadmill and I waited the long month until the results came in. My blood work was all normal, despite the nutritional abuse and neglect I had played party to. And yes, I had a slow-emptying stomach, potential ulcer, so I was told. Somehow I found that as no surprise. I was told I could continue with extensive testing or for now, limit how much food I ate at one time, sit up straight, or even lie on my right side to help the food move along.

I was given a medication for the stomach discomfort I was experiencing, which possibly was attributed to the over-the-counter analgesics I've been swallowing regularly for 16 years, and the option to change my diet. It was everything I teach my patients, everything I already knew how to do and everything I did for years. The verdict was in. It was time to move ahead with my goal and jump in now with two feet. I had run out of excuses. I couldn't even provide myself with a good enough reason to dismiss the goal I had set.

The doubt that had crept in were all based in fear. Was I strong enough to achieve this dream, to do battle with my mind, body, and spirit? Or would I allow fear to kill the last chance I had? Yes, I had run out of excuses. If I wanted the "medal with mouse ears," it was up to me. I now had to make a choice. I had to decide to face my fears, whatever they might be, as I continued on this path. It was a risk. To move forward with a full commitment, to take the chance, and just go for it. No more searching for excuses, entertaining fear and whispers of doubt. I was going for my dream, even if I was afraid.

FEBRUARY

January passed and February was calling me to the scale. I dreaded the scale. I don't own one and haven't ever in my adult life. The numbers have always haunted me. If I stand on the scale and lose weight, I would eat in celebration, of course. If I stand on the scale and gain weight, I would eat my feelings of defeat.

"Those are just numbers," I would tell myself. "Muscle weighs more than fat, so eventually it balances out and there's really no way to tell progress through the numbers game."

I had always relied on my clothing to tell the tale. But the scale was calling me. I heard it. I knew the magic number I was eventually striving for—the weight I was when I ran the New York City Marathon—125 pounds. Then, I was thin, feeling good, and the doctor had mistakenly told me my weight after I had asked him not to, when I had gone for my knee injection a week before the race.

"I can't believe you weigh so much, looking at you," he said.

"I always weigh more than I look," I answered politely, wondering why at a size 2, I was still so heavy. *"A lot of weight to carry for 26 miles,"* I thought. However, I did do it. Therefore, in my mind, that's always been the secret number, which I don't ever say aloud for fear I will sabotage myself.

I was feeling a little lighter, my clothes were just a smidge baggier, but I assumed it was all in my head. My digestion had improved by now and I attributed the lightness to my small frequent meals, reduced starch intake, and conscious increase of fiber. *Do I get on the scale?* I had been brave enough to live though the 157-pound starting point. *Could I withstand success or defeat so soon in my quest? What if I hadn't lost enough? Will I be walking forever, months on end, never being able to break into a stride and challenge my limbs? How long would I be limited to passive exercises? I have a marathon to run!! I am a runner!!*

The chanting of the tall, thin, metal beast beckoned me my entire workout the first day of February. I could hear the quiet whispers of my name being called to stand before the cold, metallic, number god.

Years of havoc and sabotage will again join me as I step onto the pallet of judgments and discover whether I was achieving any success or just spinning my wheels. I chose to stand, tall and confident after my workout, figuring the sweating I did would only work to my benefit.

Waiting until the women's locker room was empty, my longtime adversary and I met face to face for a confrontation. I stood tall, zeroed out the bar, took a deep breath, and stepped onto the cold, metal base. I immediately set the weight to 157 pounds and looked to see if the scale was still balanced. It wasn't. Okay, now to slowly slide it left towards the "lighter" side of the bar to see if it rose. Nothing. I slid it a little more to the left. "Use the power of positive thinking," I told myself and took another deep breath.

Ever so slightly, the bar started to move! I expelled a huge sigh of relief, not realizing I had been holding my breath. I continued to slowly nudge the slider weight to the left until it finally rested at 150 pounds. Seven pounds! I had lost seven pounds? That couldn't be. Something must be wrong.

I stepped off and reset the beast and stepped on again—seven pounds. I smiled a smile large enough to light up the entire locker room!! I had never smiled standing before the beast and here I was—accomplished, confident, and immensely relieved.

My plan was to keep this commitment monthly and visit my adversary. I was stronger than the metal parts which so easily judged me. I was now tougher and even more determined to find my way back to me. I was on the right path and I was going to keep walking, but soon, I promised myself, I would run.

That evening, I really felt good leaving the gym. Really, I felt like screaming, "I lost seven pounds!!" to everyone there. Instead, I walked out with a sheepish grin. My thoughts were consumed with deciding my next workout trip. I would add another piece of fitness equipment to condition me, before I could break into a stride.

My knee didn't hurt at all walking, but occasionally it plagued me in other activities. I knew the pain was not far from away. I returned to the gym the next day and stepped onto the Stepper Machine. There's the pain! I felt it right away.

"Remember, you had the surgery so you could run," the voice in my head politely reminded me. *"Walking wasn't the problem; running was. And it was only fixed so you could run at all."*

Steps are one of the daily activities that cause my knee to ache. However, I thought a controlled machine, set lightly, would be different. It was not.

Then I tried the Skier. I used to have one once, but the dragging of the leg just scraped along the inside of my knee cap like a knife. Two machines down and one more to try—the stationary bicycle. Success! I was able to pedal freely without any difficulty. Actually, it felt quite good. I felt it stretching and strengthening my quadriceps and I was able to relax a little through the workout.

Following my knee surgery, my surgeon had told me to cross-train to strengthen the tops of my legs, because the running pulls and tightens the backs of my legs. It would only work to my benefit, and so my cross-training had begun in my quest for a medal with mouse ears. I became quite well acquainted with the stationary bike.

MARCH

February flowed directly into March and I began to pick up momentum. I felt good even though I continued to have the nagging knee pain. I would be brave this month. I had lost enough weight to try and run at a slow, even pace, at least so I thought.

I started on the treadmill in my normal walking stride. *"Three minutes, that's what I'll try. Only three minutes. I'll run and I will see how it feels."* I was excited, nervous, and quite apprehensive, but I so wanted to run. I walked for five minutes and then picked one of my favorite songs from my playlist, turned up the volume, and set the treadmill to running speed. I took off.

Short strides, no sprinting, stepping each step with conscious precision, moving at a pace I hadn't experienced in years. *I was running!! It felt so good!!! I felt alive, strong, and confident.* I moved like I hadn't missed a step. It came flooding back to me like a dear old friend who was just waiting for me to call. The rhythm moved me. I felt like I was flying, like my feet were barely touching the platform! I moved with such exhilaration I almost forgot to breathe through it all. It felt like I had wings on my back and I was floating with the pulse of the run. I'm finally doing it! I have finally found myself again: *the runner.*

Three minutes is what I allowed and three minutes was all I had. I was tired, out of breath and anxious to set the treadmill back to a walking pace. I was sweating and my heart was pumping and I had a nibble of what was to come. I had found my runner-girl and she was waiting to explode and take over this body.

I walked, caught my breath for a good ten minutes and ran again, another three minutes. Releasing myself to the run, letting myself go into the flow of the energy that had been impatiently waiting inside to erupt and set me free. I let go. I ran. I ran for the first time since I could actually remember. I ran like a runner.

Saying a quiet prayer of thanks, I wiped the sweat from my face and reset the treadmill to walk. My inner runner had been set free. Now it was up to me to face what demons lay ahead. I felt ready that March day; invincible and powerful!

I am at my strongest and I believe, most days, at my best, when my body is in the rhythm of the run. I can feel the power of my spirit pulsing through me—confidence and determination push me forward with each step and each breath. I hadn't been at my best for a very long time, and it felt good to know that I could actually feel that way again. I ended my workout with my best friend next to me.

"How did it feel to run again?" she asked.

I answered, *"ME! It felt like ME!"*

THE TREADMILL

By the end of March, I decided to concede to the desires to glide freely and run regularly. I decided to stand before my challenger, which up until now has been gentle and cooperative—my challenger being the treadmill and its unforgiving demands on my body. Its potential to judge my abilities as an athlete and runner had not always been kind.

Once I attempt to run regularly, the mystery of my physical endurance will be revealed and I will have to face potential victory or failure, as my legs are tested against the values of an unforgiving machine. I felt ready, yet afraid; I so wanted to be the athlete I had been. I knew I was going to have to master my opposing adversary who until now, lay quiet and content in a walking pace, ready to push my physical, mental and emotional potential to a place I had not seen in years—and possibly deem me incapable of reaching my dream.

For now, it was the judge. I had encountered the metallic, judging beast of the scale and come away smiling. Would I be so blessed breaking into a running stride on a machine that possibly held the answer to my future?

Facing the treadmill, standing in place and stretching before pressing the start button, has always been a very humbling experience for me. Within the safety bars on either side and the panel, so colorfully lit in front, lie the truest test of my ability and tells of the sins in my past. The treadmill is non-forgiving; it is callous and harsh and is not meant to be a friend.

In the confines of the treadmill space lie a confessional for the soul, a vortex that swirls throughout and within, capturing the sins of the participant and bringing before that person whatever it is able to confiscate from their soul. The treadmill enforces a space of self-evaluation and examining self-worth.

When I stand on my chosen treadmill, I wonder as I prepare my stiff legs, what emotions will surface as I place one foot in front of the other for the selected duration. *Will it be a good run? Will I endure the miles I have mentally prepared for? Will my knee ache or worse yet, will I hurt it running?* Every step is crucial, my posture deliberate. But my mind drifts, feelings erupt, especially during the longer intervals.

The treadmill will tell if overeating and binging occurred; it will lay waste to its prey if there is a lack of fuel or fluids, thereby leaving its victim tired and fatigued. It can tell if sleep is required or if insomnia flourishes; it will reveal if days off have occurred or if the air is heavy, leaving breathing a struggle. It measures, it calculates, and it doesn't stop unless told to do so. The pace is steady and fixed.

The button is pushed and the humming begins. The belt moves slowly, awaiting my every command. In the beginning, I am in charge; I enter this space willingly, knowing its benefits for me. I choose a walking stride while I get the blood moving and my muscles loosen. For two minutes, I will have it easy. For two minutes, I will do a systems check on all moving parts, reviewing my physical being for potential cramping and stiffness before selecting my challenge.

The belt picks up and I steadily place the left foot down first, then the right, heel to toe, praying for a balanced, even gait. I continue to move with the selected pace, placing one foot in front of the other, just as the belt demands.

The motion becomes more fluent, steady and hopefully even. Sometimes I have to stop and stretch to keep my knee from hurting, just for seconds, but it does help. Then I am back on the belt, moving in rhythm with the humming and the expectation set before me, but there is more.

In the past, the mile markers usually told how my workout would likely go. My first mile always my hardest, so I know once I've past that first mile, I would probably be able to run the next two before needing a time check. Once I hit five miles, I would decide if I would continue on, all the while completing a systems check on how I'm feeling.

I have run with pain and run through pain and there have been times I just ran with pain, so I would have to stop and get off and hope the next workout day. My body had a short memory lapse and simply forgot the mishap. But there is still more to the hum of the treadmill, which quietly whispers to the soul of the one who chooses the challenge.

During the run, past the mile markers, where the mind forgets the body is running, exists a space where emotions and feelings float. The treadmill, in its unforgiving pattern, keeps the legs moving and the mind releasing into a space where vulnerability and strength collide, leaving the participant open to the thoughts and insecurities that lie within the athlete.

The treadmill is the confessional; the place where athletes release their true feelings of why they are running, where they are running to and/or what they are running from. The brain has relaxed, the right side taking control, opening the vortex of feelings that lie within. Feelings of insecurity, anxiousness, inferiority, and defeat can float above the runner, continuing the rhythm.

Achievement, accomplishment and success swirl around and it is the task of the runner to select the ones that need attention, the ones that need to be dealt with, and the ghosts that haunt. All these emotions find their way to the surface of the innocent being, setting out for a daily workout. An emotional vortex spins before the athlete, sometimes too quickly for actual evaluation; a cavalcade of emotions reflux from the soul for exposure and reflection.

It is in this moment when the runner has let go of self and allowed the soul to come forward; the moment where one-third of the runner's time is spent in the air, that a cleansing begins.

Afterward, there exists a moment where strength ensues, where the troubles of the heart have been lifted, as the belt hums and the legs select their pace. A releasing lightens whatever burdens the athlete entered with, and a letting go occurs.

I have chosen in this moment of letting go to picture myself approaching the finish line of my race. I picture in my mind's eye the final clock ahead of me and the cheering crowd fading on both sides.

This is the image I cling to, the one that keeps me moving forward. I cry, because I know that when this image materializes at the end of 26.2 miles I will feel the relief I long for. I visualize myself finishing strong and healthy, just as I feel at that moment in the confessional—forgiving myself, loving myself, finding myself, and accomplishing my dream.

Results vary daily, however. I will return to the cushioned, even platform that eases the impacts of the run, especially on tired legs. I cannot say I have laid witness to a personal runner's high. However, I can say that I feel my strongest and most confident when I am running. I am lighter, carefree and slightly indestructible when my workout is complete. I know when I wipe the sweat from my face, I am already planning my return.

I choose this course as I increase the belt speed on my treadmill. I am ready to face the outcome of my attempt to glide within the bars of the confessional and not only face the physical limitations that will present themselves, but also the thoughts and demons that will also be exposed as the left side of my brain gives way to the right during the motion of the run.

Floating into a state of self-evaluation at the hands of this machine that guarantees an evenness of rhythm and a consistency of time, allows for a unique relaxation and purging of the mind. I know what waits and I know the acceptance of the next step forward is the next step of growth. Its challenges arrive in perfect sequence along my dream's path and I must run the first mile to be able to run the marathon.

The physical and emotional baggage must be addressed and put into their proper place. The treadmill, as benign as it appears, is eager to assist with the task. Its unforgiving nature and measure of time and ability drive the desire to continue to improve and be better than the time before, all the while exposing the swirling emotional insecurities, which have up until now grounded the runner, grounded me.

Spring moved along as it always does, gently changing the cooler days into beautifully warm, sunny days, crisp with newness and hope. I remained faithful to my training regime and continued increasing my mileage ever so slightly. I was still keeping my afternoon appointment and the gym had thinned out nicely. I was no longer competing for a treadmill and my best friend went with me as often as she could.

I was running now, every day, slowly cresting at five miles, then hopping onto the stationary bike for a couple more miles. I considered my time on the bike my cool down, and my legs, especially my knee, enjoyed the forward motion and use of my quadriceps balanced the stride of my runs. My knee felt better after the biking and didn't ache as much throughout the day.

Of course, I remain diligent to icing and stretching daily, yet the nagging ache stayed with me. I had become accustomed to the fragility of my knee and pampered it, making every step deliberate and keeping to proper posture, preserving what capabilities I still had remaining to use.

I ran through the spring of 2011 with hope and an occasional heavy heart, fear lingering in the back of my mind with every step, not knowing how many miles I had left in my knee. *Was I overusing whatever rations I had left in my joint's reserve?*

I ran with pain and every so often, if I landed just right, a sharp knife shot through my knee cap. I learned to breathe through my runs a mindful, intentional breath, allowing my inner light to radiate in my legs and prayed for strong healthy runs. I tried to dismiss the fear that lightly lingered as I dealt with other insecurities that arose and challenged me emotionally. Still, I allowed the energies to flow through and embrace me.

Believing in the power of intention and the healing powers of love and light, I had begun to couple my desperate search for relief of my fears, anxieties, and physical pain with my faith, knowledge and practice of Reiki. I focused healing and relief on my body with affirmative intention, allowing the prayers to flow from my heart. I found emotional solitude with my release coming from a place of love and gratitude, centering on the gift of each individual step and appreciating the ability to have strong legs willing to carry me through my intended dream.

It is difficult to battle the fears within without faith. Faith is the armor that gives the strength and protection to move forward, so I armed myself and went into battle. I couldn't allow my emotions to use me, control me. I needed to keep them in check. I felt as though the power of intention was crisp and clear when I ran, so I learned to focus on prayers, positive ideas and objectives "Love and light I send to you my legs, my knees" when with each step, I felt a twinge of pain.

Breathing deeply and visualizing the beam expanding into my body, from my head and down into my legs I noticed that with positive thoughts, my pain eased and my running continued more easily. I also began to notice as I became more in tune to my steps and posture, if my thoughts drifted to a negative connotation, I began to feel pain more readily.

There was no cheating with my posture when it came to my knee. It felt every shift of weight, every lean forward, so my running stance became erect and balanced and there was no room for any deviation. The treadmill and I began to work together. However, I, being the more flexible of the two, always felt a flood of emotions begin once the right brain took over and assumed responsibility for the experience.

I ran through my feelings, my fears, my anxieties and my disappointments; I ran through my victories. I felt love and peace engulf me, as if my senses were magnified and slowly fine-tuned. I allowed myself to feel them *all* and I began to open up as a person and recognize the walls I had built, which reflected themselves outwardly in the significant weight gain I had previously experienced. I was tearing down those walls, my weight was coming off, and physically, I was feeling good, except for the knee. I was slowly rediscovering who I was and allowing her to surface, forgiving her and loving her.

I continued to visualize the finish line and me crossing it easily. I also started to place a small towel over my treadmill panel, one with a colorful picture of Sorcerer Mickey Mouse holding up one finger with ribbons of magic swirling around him. The reminder helped me to change my focus from the digital numbers turning and instead assisted my mind in drifting through the parks, visualizing my route and finishing strong and uninjured.

At times, I felt a cry well up within me as I acknowledged to myself I was preparing to complete my long-awaited dream. The support of the picture of Mickey Mouse draped over my tread-mill numbers, and the promise of success, helped to engage my mind during hours of inside running; breaking the monotonous pattern of my workout. He was there to remind me of the magic and blessings in my life and because I chose to run that day, I moved one day closer to the completion my dream.

I faced the tall, metal beast at the end of each month and by the last days of June, I was an accomplished 125 pounds. The flow of my run was much easier now and the weight on my frame felt comfortable. My endurance progressed and I stayed faithful with my nutrition, protein and supplement intake. If only I could move with ease and without pain.

Feverishly, I read about natural supplements to decrease joint pain and inflammation and began a natural regime of glucosamine, MSN, *Arnica montana*, and natural cherry extract. I continued with my prescribed Ibuprophen, ice, and added the supplements for support. I meditated and focused healing light throughout my body, reaching and searching for whatever would help alleviate the pain that plagued me on every run.

I focused on what I wished to see manifest in my life. I allowed myself to drift into my intentions of finishing my event, visualizing a strong, healthy race, as I respected the present moment of the treadmill run that allowed for the meditative state and the necessary physical training .

Eventually, I had begun to expect and even learned to control the flood of emotions that arose when I ran as I got to know myself again. I was appreciative of the escape and looked forward to my intimate time within the treadmill's confessional walls. All that spring, I learned to tune into the responses of my physical movements and the flow of energy within my body. I began to work with my mind to allow my thoughts a meditative space—an appreciation of the gift of a healthy body, forgiveness of my restlessness on days when I needed to rest and mentally wanted to run. I humbled myself in thankfulness for the opportunity to be able to work towards my treasured dream.

SACRIFICE

With the commitment of training for any event of duration, sacrifice is the key that unlocks the freedom of determination. Without sacrifice, it is unlikely the goal will see fruition; it takes sacrifice.

It was given much thought when I committed to my marathon year. I had forgotten, however, how deep it runs. Sure, in the past I ran races—two marathons—and the memories exist without pain and suffering.

We remember only the good—that is human nature. Just like childbirth, we rejoice in our beautiful children and forget the pain. We know there was pain, of course—it's childbirth—just as we know there's pain, and it's a marathon, so the undertaking of sacrifice about to be made in preparation for 26.2 miles can elude the training participant.

I know when I committed; I didn't strategize and plan my year of restraint and discipline. I figured I would take one step at a time and see how I things went.

My first and most prominent sacrifice was my diet. It needed a drastic overhaul and with my nagging digestive issues, it was best I concede to the small, frequent meals and higher protein intake. I increased the fluids and start looking for places to pee while I was driving while making my nursing visits. That was an inconvenience and a nuisance, and some days it was all I could do but hold it.

I gave up on the heavy meals, the high-calorie choices, and even my two favorite foods—bagels and pizza. Of course, 100-calorie bagels and a slice of pizza every now and then would cause no harm, but I love bagels and pizza! I found I needed to choose a more high-fiber carb to help with keeping my system open and regular. The bulkiness of my two favorite indulgences were not only bloating me, but slowing my system down to almost a complete stop. It's so hard to run when you feel so weighted.

Then there's the protein requirement; some foods high in protein are definitely left to an acquired taste. Powder supplements offered not only a kick to my hydration needs, but also helped my body recover from a workout and provide easy protein digestion, especially when my run was completed and my stomach wanted nothing to do with food. I felt better when I reached for a supplement drink, even though I admit, I never reached the status to say, "Wow, I can't wait for my post-run shake!!"

Second, I committed to running a 26.2-mile race on a bum knee, at the age of 49, investing my savings in myself and my family to travel hundreds of miles, to reach for my long-awaited dream.

This meant there were things in which I could no longer participate during my everyday life, removing the chance of becoming injured. For example, going into the ocean. Now the ocean at the Jersey Shore was a tad rough in the summer of 2011; jumping waves and getting smacked by the ones missed wreaked havoc on my knee. Every time I jumped and came down on my knee, every time I fell over into the water, I felt knee pain.

I was scared and disappointed and chose to remain a sand dollar on the beach and not a guppy in the water that season. Fortunately, I love the beach, so remaining on the sand and not going into the water made me a little sad, but I was secure in the knowledge that it was the right choice at the time.

Other activities that I eliminated from my spring/summer itinerary were, for example, hiking. I love a good hike or walk through paths, especially in the mountains, but the inclines and declines were just too hard on my knees. If I hadn't been in training, I would have toughed it out like I always do to enjoy the fun, but when your dream rests on whether or not your kneecap rides smoothly as you tackle a hill, a second thought becomes more than just a passing one.

Road-racing. Just a weekend run for a t-shirt and a good cause could jeopardize my entire plan. Remember, that's how I developed my ITB syndrome—participating in a race that wasn't in the plan, that disrupted nine months of running, replacing it with physical therapy and preventing me from running the Walt Disney World® Marathon the first time. Road races were out for the year; there was only one road race in the immediate future, and I was holding tight to the vision.

Shoes. No, not running shoes. Real shoes. The kind worn with business clothes, nice clothes, cute clothes; the variation of wedge on different shoes, including long-term wearing of flip-flops, wreaked havoc on my knees. The discomfort, partnered with anxiety while taking each step, keeping my posture straight and holding my breath, praying my knees survived the event of just walking, kept me wearing my running shoes most of the time and flip-flops on brief, infrequent occasions, to reach the beach sand from the parked car.

Party foods. Barbecued foods, the fatty, delicious kind, cooked outside on the grill, all summer long. I was closely watching my weight and overall health, I hadn't gotten to 157 pounds by eating right. I missed the party foods, the dips and the greasy indulgences. I steered away from those, knowing their ingestion would undeniably leave me bloated and feeling quite sluggish. I had to be light to be able to move and exercise; those fabulously delicious foods weighed me down like an anchor. I had to leave them behind in this summer in lieu of lightness.

Stairs. I was careful of what I lifted, the added weight I felt on my limbs. I was cautious of steps and their risers. As a visiting nurse in an urban environment, I face a variety of different steps and stairs daily. Each encounter required a mindful deliberation of movement, feeling each step with complete focus and balance, and a quiet prayer.

Sleeping. I relished the comfort at the end of the day that comes from a pillow at my back, a pillow at my front, two under my head and one between my legs from my knees to my ankles, so my bones don't press against each other. I was padding myself like a newborn and not easily turning in at night, but lay in soft stillness. The weight was off, and so was the extra padding of my body. I found comfort in the sleep cocoon I had created.

The daily training caused an achy, unsettling pain that reverberated through me from the constant pounding of my joints. However, relief was welcomed and my sleep undeniably improved.

August

August arrived and the flow of my running was critically interrupted one afternoon, with one step.

On the treadmill, every foot strike I made was with great precision and care. There existed no room for cheating in my gait. Any shift, especially forward, meant stabs of pain through my right knee pain.

One afternoon, during a routine run at the fitness center, my right foot came down differently and in a blink, my knee felt like it had shattered. Immediately, I looked down to see if was still attached. I reassessed and shifted my gait, ready for the next foot strike, trying to keep my shoulders back and my legs at an even stride. I landed again.

Pain, real pain! It felt like my leg had splintered into toothpicks. Another foot strike and it was worse. I couldn't run through it. I stepped off the treadmill, stretched, and turned the speed down to a walking pace.

I was nervous now. My goal of 26.2 miles seemed far into the fog. What had happened?

Immediately, I felt blindsided and knocked off my emotional balance. I walked the rest of my workout, falling into a cloud of denial and too afraid to attempt to run again. I was okay walking and so a brisk walk closed out my workout for the day. Before moving ahead with my training, I decided to have my knee medically reassessed by a sports medicine specialist, then face whatever the outcome.

For the next few days, I found I was able to comfortably return to my routine, but not in excess of a five-mile interval. Beyond the five miles, I felt this new pain return, just not as sharp.

I made appointments with my doctor, but the first available appointment was not until September. I promised myself I would go and for the time being, I would conquer easy runs with a shorter stride and a steady, even pace. I would keep my legs moving, but no further than a five-mile run.

I had also scheduled a vacation and was looking forward to the travel diversion. I promised myself a small respite while on holiday. In no way did I feel over-trained physically—in fact, quite the opposite. Mentally, the weight of my goal had become a heavy burden.

My kids were anxious to make the final reservations for Disney and I started to secretly second-guess my commitment. I felt a nice break from the daily grind would do me a world of good. We were away on vacation for eight days, and for eight nights, I did not train, count protein grams, calories or balance my intake.

Instead, I ate donuts and chocolate. I stayed up late and slept in. I did not run. However, I brought my running shoes to walk in and I also brought my flip-flops for poolside. I was not going to worry about training; I left those weights and chains home. I needed to.

I also knew the burden of the marathon commitment I chose had substantially changed my lifestyle and for eight days in August, I left it all home to rest and await my return. I was able to let go and unwind, away from the confines and structure of the training schedule that had become my life. I relaxed and had fun.

We returned home from the vacation and I followed through with the self-promise of a medical evaluation. I saw a sports medicine physician who specialized in knee joints. His conclusion was acute chondromalacia, "runner's knee," and his professional recommendation was a treatment of three intra-articular injections and physical therapy for six weeks.

I didn't need to stop my running during treatment. However, it was necessary to complete the treatments once started. I would make my appointments for September and arranged my injections to coincide with the physical therapy. The doctor stressed that many of his patients with this problem come to him because they have difficulty standing from a seated position. I was seeing him because I wanted to run 26.2 miles.

The doctor shared his sympathy for the inner runner and asked me to please consider biking once the marathon was completed. "The problem doesn't improve or heal; its only potential is to get worse," he shared.

He agreed to help me get through my upcoming event. However, his long-term recommendation for treatment was to stop the running. I left his office relieved, knowing I was going to be able to receive the help I needed and the promise of temporarily correcting the problem and the pain. I couldn't think of giving up the running, not today. Today I had to think of how I was going to now add to my schedule physical therapy, injections and increased running times.

At the end of August, the beast called. It wanted to know the truth of the month and if I had been faithful to my cause. I heard it cry loudly as I returned to the gym following my brief respite. The cold, stiff, metal monster stood alone and ready to judge. I confronted the beast by saying, "Not this month," and walked away, my head held high.

Only a few whispers were heard thereafter. Then silence. I had finally quieted the beast with my spirit, the judge of my actions, ready to reprimand. Instead, I discovered the force of my inner strength and a part of myself that was now exceptionally forgiving of my being human.

SEPTEMBER

The beginning of September met me with a new path to continue my journey. I had wrapped up the summer season and my vacation down-time, and was now faced with the final segment of my marathon training, which wouldn't be as forgiving with excuses.

I was now on an official count down. I was four months away from race day and I didn't feel nearly as far along in my conditioning and training as I would have liked. It wasn't easy balancing all of my irons in the fire and now I was faced with a timeline that demanded my utmost, immediate attention.

A mild panic floated through me as I saw my available time to train quickly dissolving. Would I be able to reach the goals I had set for myself without compromising all facets of my life? This was the month I had set aside for physical therapy and my intra-articular injections. Both were to coincide. That was the agreement I had made with my doctor and myself. I had to stick with my promise, schedule my appointments and begin the last phase of my journey.

With trepidation, I scheduled both my physical therapy and injections. My evaluation from the physical therapist would be the day before I was to be injected. My injections were scheduled for three consecutive Thursdays and I wasn't convinced the injections were the right decision for me. I was afraid of a potential adverse outcome, which might leave me unable to run at all.

How was I to know if I would have a side effect or a complication? The nurse in me nagged at the possibility and kept me questioning the choice.

Out of necessity, I also met September with a new personal training schedule. Until that point, all of my training had been done after work. For this new and last segment, I would do my training BEFORE going to work. I used to do it before, years ago, when my children were young and my schedule was tight. Somehow, I had been able to set the alarm, get out of bed early almost every morning. Then, I had small children at home!

My daily routine was easier now. Surely, I could get out of bed before work, knowing I didn't have to pack a diaper bag, bottles and snacks. I only had to pack *me*. *"A no-brainer,"* I thought.

So I set the alarm for 5am and planned my time intervals in my head. I had to be on the treadmill by a certain time to make it home by the required time to head to work. I was set, excited, and even had trouble dozing off.

Needless to say, 5am came quickly and I felt like I had hardly slept. I knew, however, this was a good choice—to schedule my workouts early.

My race would be early and I had to get used to being up and running before the sun. Plus, I love the morning and seeing the sunrise—but 5am!? That *was* early. I set the snooze for 10 min and contemplated postponing my workout for just one more day. One more day would not make a difference in the entire year of training and my body wouldn't know the difference... today.

The alarm went off and I sat up on the edge of my bed. Groggy and tired, I reached inside for the light that drives me forward. I whispered a small prayer of thanks as I stood, made my bed, and got myself together for the gym.

It was 6:15 by the time I got onto the treadmill and I was annoyed with myself for having to hit the snooze; I would have to squeeze my workout in the time I had instead of completing my workout as planned.

That first day, I ran a steady five miles and only had time for a ten-minute, three-mile bike ride. I quickly remembered how when I was younger, I was almost able to doze through my workouts, actually giving myself time to mentally wake up, and relax the left side of the brain to let the right side dominate my time in the confessional.

My emotions flowed. I felt them and let go. I focused on the finish line of the race and enjoyed one-third of my time in the air. I cried and gave thanks as I pushed forward that first September day. I knew I would excel at running in the mornings. I would enjoy clearing and cleansing my mind prior to beginning my workday. I discovered I wasn't as sore as I had become while training in the afternoons. Still, each step was careful and deliberate.

Slowly but surely, my morning workouts began to flow, one after the other. The commitment was a conscious one and every day, there was a minor discussion in my head when the alarm went off. "What should I do? Get up or hit the snooze?"

Eventually, I was able to develop a ritual for myself and a new regular routine, which afforded me the benefit of bringing to my physical therapy evaluation a training program I securely had in place. I could introduce myself as a runner, in training for a marathon. It felt good to be so confident in myself.

The day before my evaluation arrived and I spent a nervous 45 minutes trying to find a parking spot on the streets in South Philadelphia. I just barely made it in at 2pm and quickly filled out the necessary paperwork. My heart beat more quickly as I waited anxiously for my physical therapist.

To my surprise, he was a runner and we hit it off immediately. He took the time to understand and evaluate the pain and discomfort that plagued me, and which was holding me back both physically and emotionally. I shared that I had been spooked by the recent "fracturing" episode on the treadmill. I was genuinely afraid to run past a comfortable five miles a day. I also shared the dreadful news of the minimalist views of the doctors I had visited and the love I had for both running and completing the Walt Disney World® Marathon.

My physical therapist surprised me by sharing that he had also always wanted to run the Walt Disney World® Marathon.

He would do everything he could to help me gain the proper alignment and strength to reach my dream. We talked and shared for over an hour; he evaluated and instructed and sent me home with home exercises and stretches to complete daily. I scheduled a subsequent session with him the following week and completed my home regime as directed.

I also chose to postpone my injections until further notice. If I found a natural resolution to my chronic pain and discomfort without the injections, I was content. I could choose the injections at any time; the physical therapy was now and I planned to seize the moment and benefit fully from the opportunity before me.

I dutifully performed my exercises and went through the performance plan; I completed the stretches as prescribed and continued to run, before work, five days a week. Mornings were becoming easier and my internal clock had begun to adjust to the time shift.

Oh, yes, there were mornings I just couldn't get out of bed. There were mornings I would wake with the alarm or others an hour earlier. On those mornings, I would slip downstairs and make myself a cup of coffee, then slide back between the sheets, sipping the warm brew, waking myself up slowly. I also found this quiet time afforded me time to reflect, meditate and give thanks before starting my day. Some days, this plan worked. Other days, my body or mind just said, "No, not today," and I dozed off, conceding I needed the rest. Then I was left to readjust my entire week's workout strategy.

I continued to go to physical therapy weekly and through my individualized exercise program, I discovered that my painful right leg was considerably weaker than the left. I began a light weight-training program to increase my leg strength and balance, which I hadn't realized were even an issue. I learned that I was able to perform pain-free as long as I committed to the stretches and the planned regime. I was improving and I was feeling good and for the first time in years, I was moving and climbing and running with ease.

The anxiety about my physical ability to run started to wane and my confidence grew. Along with that, my long run crested at a painfree ten miles. With the encouragement and support of my physical therapist and the progress I had made, by the end of September, I felt like I might actually run my marathon without too much damage. I was on course, suffering less and becoming stronger. I continued to visualize the finish line, stepping on the timing mat, and crossing healthy.

With the increase in my running intervals, my physical therapist decided it was time to attempt running outside. It made complete sense. My race was outside and eventually, I knew deep down, I was going to have to attempt the pavement and its impact on my limbs. I was definitely stepping out of my comfort zone and off of the softer, more forgiving treadmill belt.

My physical therapist promised my gait and posture would be different outdoors and that I might actually find it more comfortable once I began running outside. I promised that when

October arrived, I would head out the door and onto the streets—another test to pass along my journey.

I would gather the fragments of my fears, identify them one by one, and leave them behind when the time came to venture out my front door. I needed to be brave and let them go.

It had been two months since I faced the beast—the scale. I could hear it calling to me a whole week before the end of September. It would have to wait until the last day for our confrontation. I was not going to appease the calling by appearing one day early.

I wasn't sure where my weight had landed after the month of vacation and eating, and a month of therapy and shorter distances. I had been faithful to my current plan and training, but I wasn't feeling any lighter. If anything, I felt heavier, so I wasn't anxious to stand in judgment until the very last day.

When September 30 arrived, I stood ready to be weighed. The calling was relentless and by now, I just wanted to get it over with. I stood before the cold, steel beast and zeroed out the bar, making sure all readings would be accurate. Then, with a deep breath, I stepped on. First, I slid the 100-pound weight to its proper place. Easy. Deciding to meet the task head on, I slid the individual pound bar right to 125 pounds, expecting the bar to float evenly, determining my current and unchanged weight. It didn't move; the bar remained still. *What?! This can't be, could it?*

Over the two months of not getting weighed, could I have actually gained weight? I knew I deviated a little from my normal intake regime, but I also had a whole month after the fact of training! In disbelief, I slid the pound bar to the right, waiting until it landed on 128 pounds. I had gained three pounds.

Stunned, I stepped off the scale and viewed myself in the full-length mirror. My immediate response was: "I'm going backwards!" I'm supposed to be taking off the weight, not putting it on! The more I weigh, the more I have to carry 26.2 miles. I likened the extra weight to carrying a 5-pound bag of sugar. Yes, it's "only" five pounds, but if you have to carry the bag 26.2 miles, it will get heavy, real quick.

Respectfully, I left the beast and went into the workout area. My mind reeling from the setback, I started my five-mile run.

With my favorite music in my ears and the harmony I have made with the treadmill, I came to terms with my results. It is said that muscle weighs more than fat. I've never actually read the research, but it seems to be a common reality among those attempting the weight game.

As I ran, virtually pain-free, remaining faithful to my stretches and weight training, I decided to let it go. I am stronger now, two months after my last weigh-in. I am running farther and have reached the place where my legs, on most days, feel better when they are running, than when they are not. I have grown as a runner and as an individual. Maybe muscle really does weigh more than fat and I need the muscle to carry my frame along all 26.2 miles.

No matter how the thoughts spun in my head, the outcome before the beast didn't change. I took a deep breath, let go of the fear that whispered, and as I ran that day, I discovered that I was deeply thankful—thankful for the realization that the results didn't signify a failure, but rather a success.

My stride continued as I ran through the thoughts of disappointment into the light of peace and accomplishment. I forgave myself during this bewildering run for fixating on who I am and the effects I am achieving, on the adages of the beast and the numbers it showed me. I opened my heart completely to the feelings of love and pride in the person I had become this final September day. I felt myself become lighter as I ran, and the heaviness of disappointment dissipate.

With each step, I realized I was a stronger, more confident person than when I started this journey and for that alone, I was grateful. I finished my run and walked past the beast without fear and despair. Instead, I held my head high. I had truly let go of the negative feelings resulting from our confrontation and the beast knew it. It also knew it would no longer call my name and occupy my thoughts; its power had dissolved and I had grown from the trials. I was moving on, past the control of the beast into a healthy, self-assured, courageous woman who was ready to begin the last stretch of her journey without the anchors of pain, fear, and failure looming behind the numbers on a scale.

October

Thoughts of running outside loomed over October like a dark, gray cloud I found I couldn't shake. The fear of my legs pounding the pavement caused me such trepidation that I actually took a week off from running. I stayed with my stretches, my nutritional regime, but I physically and emotionally removed myself from the obstacle that stood before me.

What was the matter with me? I used to love running outside. It was my outlet, my freedom and on most days, my sanity. Now I was so afraid to have come so far in my quest for my medal that I couldn't handle another setback.

My family and I were looking at plane fares. My race was coming up quickly and the fear rose in front of me like a huge mountain that wouldn't budge. I tried desperately to reason it through and muster up the nerve to head out the door. Not only had I not run outside since my iliotibial band injury, but I had stopped running altogether, gained three more pounds and was sliding ever so quickly off of my routine and training schedule.

Panic started to whisper in my ear and I knew that I had to set a date, an immediate goal, to regain my focus and return to my training; I set a target point—in three days, I would run. I hadn't decided yet if it would be outside, but in three days, I would return and continue on my marked path; I needed the three days to regroup and start over.

It was autumn in New Jersey. It was also an Indian summer with temperatures projected to reach the 80s by midday. No excuse not to run; the weather was beautiful. The leaves had begun to change into beautiful hues of red, yellow and gold. Everything was in my favor, except the fear of failure and disappointment.

I was afraid to step out of my front door and begin pounding my legs on the concrete for the first time in years. I was so beside myself, so twisted and growing more distressed each day. I felt as though I couldn't find my balance, my center. That thought just knotted itself up within me. I couldn't reason through the panic of potential failure and realization that I might not be able to handle running on concrete pavement and therefore, not be able to run my race. Where was my center? My confidence? My strength?

My fear blocked my peace and stole my joy. I wrestled with the challenge that awaited my participation. Sensing my frustration and restlessness, my best friend looked at me and said, "Let's go to the beach; take whatever is eating at you and leave it there. The ocean will take it away." And so, during the weekend of our New Jersey Indian Summer, the two of us packed up and headed to the ocean so I could find my way out of myself.

Once on the shore, the breeze was refreshing and the sun bright and warm. It was even warmer than we anticipated, and the ocean was clear and calm. I took off my shoes and socks and waded into the cool ocean water and watched as the waves washed over my feet, caressing me gently. I felt a calm embrace me. I took a deep breath of the rich, salty air, allowing it to fill my senses, my soul, and my thoughts. I released it and took another deep inhalation, feeling present and thankful. I exhaled slowly as I could feel my doubts and my fears race to the exhalation. I relaxed in the gentleness of the waves and welcomed the soft sand beneath my feet caressing my toes

It was then that I was able to find my center. It was then that I let go. I let go of the fears that had begun to cloud my thoughts and ambitions and released them into the peaceful receiving ocean. Her kindness seemed eager to receive my worries and replace them with the calm of her heart. Mother Earth rocked and stroked me as I regained the focus that had become so clouded, so lost.

Finally, I was able to open my heart and enjoy the autumn sun on my face. I knew in that moment that I had to venture outside for the next chapter of my training. That knowing came from deep within and with a quiet, intentional breath, I completely released my fears. There at the beach, I left the gray cloud of doubt that had begun to consume me and watched it transform and dissipate into the ocean air.

Soon I would find my feet on the pavement and hold my head up high to what my results would be. I would be brave and trust myself. I would follow my intentions and my training. I would proceed toward my goal with a fearless heart.

Running Outside

Running outside is definitely not the same as running on the treadmill. I believe the pair are polar opposites. I had forgotten what running outside truly entailed and when I ventured out on the morning of my day off, I was pleasantly delighted in the freedom I had forgotten existed. As I dressed in the morning, I had to remember my outside routine and the various items I might need or leave behind.

I was going to rough it today and leave water outside on my porch rather than carry it along. My plan was to circle back to the house. I would be ok. I slid on my ID band and put on my music.

Stepping out into the bright sunshine, I felt every bone and muscle. With every step, I was becoming acquainted with the ground. "One foot in front of the other," I said in my head. " I can do this!" I thought, as I continued to move gently into a rhythm, repeating my mantra: "Love and light to my legs. I'm breathing in love and light." As I repeated these words in my head, I visualized love and light beaming through me.

Beyond my initial thoughts and intentions, I suddenly noticed that I was running, easily and without pain. My feet took to the street as if they never had left and I was free. I felt the cool morning breeze against my face and smelled the dampness of the ground. I turned up my music, found my stride, and took off running. I had forgotten what a different, yet challengingly free experience being outside offered. I could zone, but still had to be aware, which is really a cool feat if you can pull it off right.

All those intervals within the confines of the indoor confessional prepared me for occupying my mind while remaining alert. I had learned to turn off the left brain and dwell in the right, yet remain in the body while floating through my run. I repeated my mantra frequently and whenever I felt a twinge of pain, I stopped and completed my stretches. I negotiated acorns, rocks, sand, wet leaves, curbs, uneven sidewalks, cars, dogs, bugs, traffic lights, and inclines (something I hadn't attempted in years).

Sometimes I think the reason running initially appealed to me was because it actually gave me an excuse to be outside. As adults, it's not usually the first thing on the to-do list. Sure, we attend our family picnics, barbecues and take our children to their soccer meets and baseball games, but what activity do adults do outside for themselves?

As children, we always played outside, sometimes until the street lights came on, and yet as adults, our lives rarely include a regular outdoor endeavor. And how beautiful it is to be outside! Connecting with the elements and one's self. I truly believe the lack of the fresh air and sunshine attributes to the confines of adulthood and its associated restraints.

To say I've discovered the secret to interminable youth would be ridiculous. However; to say I discovered what contributes to the joy in my life … I affirm the admission with a heartfelt "YES!"

Outdoors, there are no boundaries, no rules, just movement, wide-open space, breezes, warm sunshine and cool rain. There are no confines like the confessional, no numbers counting, lights blinking, or endless humming.

I had forgotten what it was like to take foot to the streets. It felt so amazingly wonderful! I had forgotten the taste of the fresh air and how the ability to really be alive emanates the soul's energy, which magnifies and releases as the body moves. On a beautiful day, when the sun is bright, not hot, and it glistens off the water, and a gentle breeze brushes against my face—it is in that moment that my soul connects with the Divine and bears witness to joy.

ELEMENTS

The miracle of the mind-body-spirit connection actualizes in the motion of the outside run. In this interlude, there are no hums, numbers, times, or platforms. Instead, there is a connection to the earth with every step. Feeling the energy of life and breathing the fresh, clean air wisps away at the heaviness of the runner, the burdens carried. Lightness develops and the soul releases itself to the ethereal wave as the body moves in the current of the universe, flowing through the run and expanding outward.

Instead of the intimate swirl of individual energy around the body, trapped in the hand bars of a machine, the energy expands outward and away, allowing a runner to be free and undefined. No numbers or speeds are present to dictate the pace, but the inner cue of the run itself sets the rhythm.

The senses, heightened in the moment, are aware of every little detail, yet somehow absorbed into the experience. It is as if the body and all its wisdom becomes attuned to every detail and receives the environment with an uncanny sharpness and bombards the participant with plethora of sensations.

So many scents and aromas—the smell of grass, dirt, flowers, trees, fragrances that attract and even odors that repel.

Some remind runners of their childhood and the excitement of being outside. Still others are new and inviting, and encourage the runner to a quicker step. All senses are intensified, barraging the participant with a keenness of possible thoughts lost.

A myriad of sounds can still be heard and acknowledged above the earphones. The steps of the runner are the loudest of all, striking the pavement with an even connection to the receiving ground; no pounding or echoing as on the treadmill, yet the softness is heard with crisp sharpness. The resonances of the surroundings, finding their way to the runner, alerting, protecting and identifying the space, almost like antennae receiving the energy waves—a dog barking, a car starting, noises that resonate past the earphones into the mindfulness of the partaker and protect the body as it moves in rhythm with the run. The noises surround and are heard, but don't distract from the oneness felt.

The softness of breathing communes with the life source and inviting the participant's focus into the present moment. The sound is peaceful, yet secure, as it continues in the flow, gentle, but heard firmly by the soul. The motion of the body continues, and the colors surrounding the athlete become brighter and sharper in the light, yet blending and melting together in the dark.

At dusk or dawn, in just the right light, the runner, relaxing the eyes, looking down at the body, can see the mystical glow of the energy field surrounding the body. As the heat and energy radiate, the soft, white glow becomes significant and bears witness to the soul that dwells within.

As the run becomes longer, bleariness comes to the eyes and reliance on the other senses engages. The runner can then meditate and allow for the passage of thoughts, prayers and resolutions to be present and peacefulness to encompass.

* * * * *

I had forgotten what miracles exist while running outside, how easy it is to let things go, releasing and communing with the beauty ever present in the moment. I had forgotten how to drop worries and concerns along the pathway for dissipation into the air. I feel my spirit at its strongest when I am running outside. I feel empowered and my connection to the power of intention is fierce and strong as I focus positive, thoughtful visualization with each step.

My heightened senses are in tune with my body and the ambiance, demonstrating a rare and remarkable experience. No wonder children always smile while they are running. Their thoughts are carefree as they enjoy living in the moment of their activity, their play, their run, their joy.

I breathed in the air and soaked in the sun—and I survived. I completed my five miles easily. When I returned home, I gave thanks for the beautiful day, the erupting memories of being outside, the peace I found within, and the fears I had finally conquered.

The next morning, my left hamstrings were extremely tight and I could definitely feel the change in surface in both my legs.

They were quite stiff and the back of my left leg had a nagging pain. I couldn't quite feel it to rub it, and I even had difficulty finding a stretch that relieved it. Nevertheless, I was up early and heading to the fitness center for my scheduled 6am treadmill run, which I accomplished without much difficulty.

I still had the nagging sharp pain and as the morning wore on and my left leg became increasingly tight. I continued with my stretches and even iced the back off my leg as I drove to work. By the end of the afternoon, I was stiff, sore and concerned. I should not be feeling so affected by my outside run this long after, so decided to take the next day as a rest day.

For my next workout, I promised myself a light three-mile run on the treadmill to keep my legs loose and hopefully limber. As it turned out, it wasn't so easy. I stretched as my new routine called for and then started walking on the treadmill for six minutes, twice as long as usual, just to get up the nerve to break into a stride.

Carefully, I bumped up the speed, placed my incentive towel with the picture of Sorcerer Mickey Mouse swirling around magical dust and holding up the Number 1 over the control panel. Then I set my music to one of my favorite songs and went all out, running at my normal pace. Well, I should say I *tried* running at my normal pace.

My left hamstrings seized into a tight cramp and my right leg felt painfully twisted. No matter how much I struggled, I couldn't get my legs to run in rhythm. It felt as though I was running on someone else's legs and didn't know how to work them! I paused, reset the treadmill to a walk and stepped off. I completed my stretches again, then I got back on and walked another three minutes. Then I rebooted the treadmill to running speed and tried again.

I know how to run, I've been doing it for months now, but my current attempts left me trying to operate legs that felt borrowed and twisted. In sheer amazement and disbelief, I set the treadmill to "walk" and walked a very long, uneventful three miles.

What could have happened? I kept playing things over in my head. I ran outside. The next day, I ran inside on the treadmill. Then I rested. Normal, not unusual and completely within my training regime. I decided to email my physical therapist with my dilemma and wait patiently for a response. My legs ached through the day, especially the right one. Still I stayed with my stretches and my routine.

My physical therapist replied around midday and told me that outside, I was using different muscles than on the treadmill. He went on to say that if I am not experiencing knee pain, not to worry about it and plan to run again. *Really? Not worry about it?*

It was true. I wasn't experiencing any knee pain, on either knee. So, beginning with a deep breath, blind trust and faith tucked in my pocket, I headed out the door the next day, a beautifully cool, fall afternoon and ran like I was meant to run, pain-free and relaxed. I finally let go of the last pieces of doubt, watching them break and fall from my soul onto the ground. I left them behind and kept running. I kept running toward my goal, running toward the finish line that awaited me, running toward my dream.

October was littered with beautiful days, dark mornings and the whisper of winter in the air. I again switched my routine to running after work so that I could run outside, just before sunset when the temperature was at its warmest.

On weekends, I ran longer runs, enjoying the morning sun. I had begun to just relax into my own rhythm, tackling inclines, avoiding tree branches, dogs, and cars, and develop an inner peace that settled within as I moved through the flow of the run.

I ran fewer days with longer stints and enjoyed my rest days as a necessary element of my training. It was a delicate strategy that required my full attention. I had to plan my meals, my work time, my rest time, my appointment calendar, and also hope the weather cooperated. Otherwise, it was back to the drawing board and a new weekly proposal.

I completed my first long run outside by mid-month, twelve miles in two and a half hours and I felt accomplished.

The days passed and the weather started to take a gentle turn towards cold. One day, it even snowed. By month's end, it was a crisp 32 degrees on the morning of my final long run of October: 13.1 miles in two hours and forty-five minutes. I knew I wouldn't be setting personal records, PRs, any time soon. However, tired and smiling, for the first time in ten months, I returned home feeling, *"I've got this!"*

NOVEMBER

N ovember's weather started with a chill; my outside running took place every two days. I found I recovered best with a day or two rest period. I could definitely feel the difference on my joints running outside, the aches and stiffness were more prevalent, so the days I ran, I continued to run longer times. I practiced with gels, sports drinks, socks, shirts, gloves and hats, attempting to assemble the system that fit me best.

It can be a tricky thing balancing the body's needs and hoping it doesn't reject things back at you with nausea, vomiting, or diarrhea. The longer the duration of my runs, the more I had to fine-tune my approach to what my body needed.

I made sure I had my bananas ready for daily consumption. I just always felt better with a banana on board, "comfort food" to prevent cramps and supply nutrition without a lot of fiber, and they are easy to digest and very portable.

In addition, I focused on hydration and nourishing my muscles with a variety of available products, continuing to search for the most profitable combination.

My legs were at the point where they actually felt best when I was running. My body had changed and it began to accept the longer runs and increased miles. Everyday activities did not provide enough exercise and motion to heed the aches and pains from my lower extremities. My legs easily became stiff, a common side effect of marathon training. Stretching was a daily necessity to maintain my flexibility and motion. I was becoming weary of the grind of training and the juggling of my schedules, the demands on my physical body with its increasing soreness, my diet with its multiple restrictions.

And insomnia had found its way into my bedroom, a side-effect of potential over-training. I continued sleeping with a pillow at my lower back, one between my legs to prevent my knees and ankles from touching each other, and one at my chest to support my front and shoulder. This is what I found most comfortable and it did lend itself to an easier night's sleep.

The weight I had lost took with it any hopes of cushioning and my muscles and bones were quite exposed. Tucking myself into my cocoon prevented any occasional spasms and supported my body during sleep, padding my joints and creating a softness that many evenings I couldn't wait to feel.

The insomnia plagued me in spurts and when it did, it created a gap in which night eating and pacing found a home. I battled the sudden awakenings and discovered my daily practice of meditation, coupled with days of no running, were the key to my relaxation and stability during this last stretch of training.

I learned to forgive myself when I scheduled days of rest. I knew I had a huge event approaching quickly, in less than two months. I also realized that with the constant stress of training and maintaining my current work schedule and family obligations, I was slowly and surprisingly becoming disenchanted with the sacrifices and demands. I found myself wishing it would just be over with.

Longer running periods that needed to be done outside, in the cold New Jersey air and with the hectic holidays approaching, I knew I had to keep a tight hold on my weight and my time management. I was not beginning my training, I was supposed to be picking up speed and running longer and easier, preparing and planning to stand on the starting line.

I was running without knee pain, staying faithful to my stretching program and my dietary intake. Nevertheless, my legs were sore and stiff and I had to ice them after every run. It seemed I was finally becoming a finely oiled machine with my rhythm and my training, yet it was taking more and more energy to get out the door. I was afraid I had trained inappropriately and reached my peak too soon, but that couldn't be. *"I'm only at the half way mark in my distance training."*

Therefore, I planned my rest days and I planned my workouts, freeing time on my calendar and convincing myself that the longer stints outside made up for the one less day that week of running. I was still logging the same number of miles, if not more, with my runs, and I was just hoping my theory would hold together come race day.

Once out the door, I slipped into a meditative run, which allowed the mental and emotional release I had become accustomed to. I needed the escape to keep my mind and body motivated for the continued weeks of running I was facing. I needed to stay focused and the visual of me accomplishing my dream would shine through the run as a beacon to follow. Nevertheless, I was feeling every bit my age and planning every day with the intention of reaching the one goal that was now driving my entire existence.

Throughout the month of November, I'm embarrassed to say, I initially struggled with getting out of the door to run. It became necessary to set aside time to complete my long runs, so without having to squeeze them into my already busy schedule, I decided to take a few random personal days off from work, with the sole resolution of running. It seemed the definite intention to have the day off just to run long, helped me focus and relax in completion of my goal.

I reminded myself throughout my session, "All I have to do today is run..." and the self-encouragement kept my legs moving and my mind free to enjoy the experience. Those specific mornings, I slept in a little, meditated and took my time getting myself together. I moved at a relaxed pace, the kind used on vacation. I practiced intentional breathing and took my time preparing for my long run. I made sure I gave thanks for my day off, my healthy body, and the opportunity to be able to run. I treated my time with respect and savored each minute as a gift, instead of rushing through the experience just to get it done.

I found that treating my long run with reverence and respect, and I enjoyed my time alone and relaxed as the flow of energy strengthened and moved within me. I learned to be still in the present moment and understand that there is time for everything that needs to be done. It is just as important for me to relax and enjoy a cup of coffee as it is to throw in a load of wash, or write a report or complete a long run.

By month's end, I had grown. I had wrestled with discontent to come full circle into the light of appreciation and blessings. I have come so far in my journey. Now I found myself in a place I wasn't even sure was possible to obtain eleven months ago. The heavy albatross of negative emotions, doubts, and fears I felt around my neck, challenging me each time to run over and over again in a monotonous cycle, wondering about the importance or significance of in it all finally lifted and flew away like a graceful dove. Lighter and enlightened to the value of being able to move with grace in a healthy body, I was able to give thanks for the blessings encircling me, to spend my intimate time alone with my soul and to find peace within, so to keep focused on achieving my goal.

I found confidence in the determination I needed to move to the next level of training. Through the tiredness and soreness, the hours spent on the road and the aches that robbed my sleep, I found within the drive to continue to move away from negative thoughts and self-talk and enjoy my gift of being able to run and continue my quest toward my long- awaited dream.

December

December began with the countdown to my race and the month was set to be busy. I faced one more long run before race day and I have to admit, I was tired. I was running longer runs on my days off from work, outside in the cold, winter air, then an hour or two recovering, which severely cut into life's daily routine.

The holiday season with its festivities and commitments, along with my longest run yet, stood before me. I definitely looked forward to my race taper and slowing down.

I planned my long run on the weekend, one month prior to my race. I set out with the expectation I would be out a good bit of the morning. I set out my water, Gatorade and gels on my porch for when I circled around in my loop and also added a few gels in my running pack for my mid-run boost. I donned my hat, gloves, music, lip balm, inhaler, running pack, layered my shirts, and laced my new running shoes. Then I headed out into the 30-degree weather. Thank goodness Florida, where the race would be run, was warm this time of year.

Immediately the cold, crisp air hit my face and lungs. My eyes began to tear and I continued running through bleary, tired eyes. Mentally, I was prepared for the long haul. I was planning at least a 3½-hour run, significant to my current long run status, yet still lacking in the training realm.

I started on my usual path through the local golf community and easily drifted into the meditative state I had become accustomed to. The music played in my ears, but I really didn't hear it. It moved my body along with its quick and familiar rhythm, but my mind was drifting. Drifting from the cold that was embracing my face, drifting from the turns and steps in the sidewalks and driveways, drifting to the place of peace, comfort, and myself.

I must have really needed this run, because the speed at which I switched from left side to right was swift and smooth. As I ran, tears streamed down my cheeks; first due to the cold, then because I was crying. "I mustn't cry, because then I will have trouble breathing," I whispered to myself. But the tears came.

This was my last long run before I was to stand at the start of my dream. My goal was only a month away. My legs were moving, and my mind swimming with emotions that needed an outlet with my race just days away. I could also feel my spiritual strength increasing and my life force growing stronger as I continued the quest.

The power of intention is so strong for me now when I run. I feel the life force erupting within my solar plexus and emanating outward. My focus moves smoothly to what I want to achieve; I visualize myself crossing the finish line, receiving my medal and feeling healthy and strong.

I visualize the same for my son, who was embarking on his first-ever race, the half-marathon. I cry some more, allowing myself to be engulfed in the feelings of the moment. My daughter, the student, first tackling her two half-marathons, 13.1 miles, in both the Disneyland Half-Marathon and the Disney Princess Half-Marathon in the Disney Coast-to-Coast Race Challenge last year, and now my son, the baseball player, with the mindset of a sprinter, is about to challenge his first race, a half-marathon, the day before mine.

Concern fills me, yet I am focused on the positive strength and visualization I have for his moment in the racing sun. I am so proud of my children, who on their own have chosen to venture into the curiosity and challenge of running. I have watched them grow, stay focused, and become better people as they and accomplish their athletic goals.

So, with each step of this final, long run, I give thanks for the blessings I have been given, the joy I have in my life and the opportunity to seek and live out my dream with the people I love standing alongside of me, tasting the very fabric of what it takes to push yourself to the limit and grow from it.

I continue to run, feeling strong and healthy and focusing my inner intentions on the Divine and connecting with the oneness that is so open to me in this moment. I no longer feel the cold. My eyes have adjusted and my heart soars with excitement and anticipation for my dream, almost close enough to touch. I keep fast to the positive images in my thoughts and join them with prayers for strength and of thanksgiving. The music plays and my feet continue and I have found my rhythmic pace, gliding me along into my second and then third hour of movement.

I circled back as planned, refueled, rehydrated, and reenergized. Then I set out for my final hour. I felt tiredness and stiffness settle in. My pace was slower and my body sprouted minors aches here and there. I intended to complete the hour and conclude my goal for the day and offer it up as my final attempt to move my training along, but the last half hour had slowly begun to take its toll.

My legs had begun to tighten, although I stretched frequently, the ileotibial band on my left leg had begun to burn, which was the same issue that kept me from running this race the first time I entered. I felt the heaviness of my legs and the hardness of my choice surface with every effort I was making. I stopped moving to stretch, both my right knee and left ITB. No complaints for my right knee, however, the burn was persistent in my left leg and I decided to end my run just at the 3½ hour mark with ice to both lower extremities as a reward.

Concern grew, and I was haunted by the old injury that had not surfaced until now. I was in the home stretch of my training. I couldn't let this issue take me out of the race again! Not when I was this close to it. I promised myself that I would stretch more and run shorter intervals. I will begin my taper and guard my legs dearly, sending healing light and positive thoughts.

As the month pressed on, I found myself completing my stretches and shorter runs to keep my legs moving, but December brought with it holiday duties, time constraints and the usual festivities encroached on most of my free time. I had hoped my body wasn't taking notes. I was hoping it wasn't counting the days, which were moving at the speed of light toward the holiday season and that it didn't notice my taper ended up not so much a taper, but a "drop off."

I hadn't run at all; I couldn't find the time. I was so busy at work, at home—shopping, baking cleaning, planning. I prayed my body wasn't logging the days missed, but felt the wisp of time as quickly as my mind did. I felt my dream barreling toward me like a quiet, definite tsunami. I couldn't see it yet, but I felt it coming.

My family was so excited for our trip to the Walt Disney World Resort—all of us planning and preparing as we celebrated our holidays, knowing we were leaving just days after.

Insecurity and doubt whispered in my ear often, as I could feel my palms sweat at the thought of 26.2 miles. Yes, I had prepared and yes, I was able to focus and run, but I also know what 26.2 can do to a person. I know the torture that incurs and the pain endured. I know that in less than two weeks' time, I would be standing at the beginning of a life- changing event, one that I had dreamed of, prepared for twice before, and now set to conquer.

I have an old advertisement in my closet. It is a street sign that reads, "To Hell and Back, 26.2." I have it hanging next to my race route on the wall. "To Hell and back"—that's where I was going and I knew it. I have dreamed of this for years and now I can honestly say that standing this close to my dream, I could feel my feet getting cold and the anxiety of failure attempting to take up residence in my mind. The fleeting thought of *What if I can't finish?* denies me its presence when I'm running and is blocked through my positive intentions and prayers.

I feel I am my strongest emotionally when I run, my most peaceful during my prayers, and the happiest place I have ever been is the Walt Disney World Resort. I have all three in my pocket and my dream within reach, with the love of my family embracing it with me. I am human, doing the best I can with what I've got. I have also grown over these past twelve months to be the person I want to be, as I move into the next stage of my life.

Yes, I will have insecure thoughts. I've decided and have learned to forgive myself for them. However; I also know that I am capable of not entertaining their presence, but moving past them to the positive in the present moment and the excitement of the richness of my life.

It takes a little self-discussion to find my way out of the cloud of doubt and fear, but the light seen, once out of the cloud, is bright and beautiful, its warmth comforting and calming, granting the mind and spirit the ability to focus and be strong.

Thus, I moved through the latter part of December battling my insecurities, while moving my mind, body, and soul to the focus of the dream ahead, the beauty of the present moment, and the excitement of experiencing a life-changing event I have so longed to do.

The Start

T ime flew as the holidays concluded, and my dream approached. The excitement in my house was uncontainable and we all were like children awaiting Santa's arrival. This would be the first vacation with my children post-divorce and my first trip back to the Walt Disney World Resort. It was a trip a year in the making—mentally, physically, emotionally, and financially. We all looked forward to a change of scenery, especially to "the happiest place on earth."

We as a family believe Walt Disney's dream; we believe that if you wish for something, it will come true. Here, the power of intention at the most innocent level exists in the place "where dreams are made" and I was going there to do just that.

The morning of our departure was surreal. I went through the motions with anticipation and disbelief. I was beginning the last leg of my journey, yet I couldn't actually focus. I had practiced "staying in the moment" and had also offered the intention in quiet prayer. I didn't want to disengage mentally; I wanted to experience it all. Nevertheless, I found myself only going through the motions of navigating the airport and the shuttle to our hotel. It was not until we were actually in the Walt

Group hug before we begin race weekend—son
Joe, daughter Stephanie, and the author.

Disney World Resort did the cloudy film lift from my vision. It was then I felt grounded in the present moment with my dream and my quest only days away.

The Florida weather was calm and inviting and it felt so good to finally be in the sunny glow and arriving on the Walt Disney World Resort property. My heart skipped a beat as the feeling of home and comfort embraced my spirit. I was in my element, in a place where dreams coming true are anticipated and even, on some level, expected. My soul knew this.

There would be no judgments, no criticisms—only the freedom to relax and enjoy being. I knew I had selected the proper place to fulfill and complete my dream of a lifetime. I knew the combination of my dream, the accomplishment of the 26.2-mile quest and reparation of a fractured person would meld together in this magical place, and assist me in becoming the person I was meant to be. I was at the Walt Disney World Resort—not only to enjoy, but also to heal, grow and leave behind the baggage I had been carrying. It was here that I would finally glue together the pieces that had been laid in place in Sedona and move on to a life patiently awaiting my arrival. I knew this transformation was upon me and I intentionally wanted to remain fully present as I experienced what was to come.

We checked into our hotel, dropped our luggage in the room, and immediately headed for Epcot with childlike excitement and anticipation. We took our time walking there, digesting our surroundings and taking in the sites. The day was beautiful and bright, the air fresh and cool and the reflection of the clouds danced atop the water along our path.

The energy was wonderful and I immediately felt at ease walking with my family. I felt myself relaxing, breathing, and being fully present. My prayer was answered. As I began to relax and stroll, absorbing my surroundings, I finally felt my emotional guard drop away.

Then, suddenly and without warning, I experienced a pressure pushing me from behind. I stopped and stood in place as I felt the push of all my efforts and sacrifices of the past year charging at me like a freight train at full speed, the whistle blowing with panic, becoming louder with each breath and the actuality of *WHY* I was really here announcing itself, mixing together as one force. The substantial physical requirements, the emotional toll it would take, and the pain I was about to endure, physically, mentally and spiritually dawned on me. I stood still and breathed, awaiting the pending impact.

I was expecting anxiety and panic upon contact, but instead, when the force struck, the ghosts of my burdens disseminated into a dark gray cloud, which delicately engulfed my physical presence in a swirl of dizziness. It embraced me, lightened, and then floated away. In that moment, my soul finally faced and released all my preparation encumbrances. The challenges and obstacles that had caused anxieties since last January, willingly dissipated into the ethers.

I was not expecting the moment; it didn't warn me nor did it linger. I felt lighter and was truly thankful and at peace, free to enjoy my time with my family at the Walt Disney World Resort, and free to keep my focus on my goal.

My family and I walked through the parks relaxed and enjoyed our time together. The challenges and excitement of the pending races kept a close pace to my son and me as we attempted to stay distracted and in the current experience to allay any apprehensions that waited just outside us.

I was concerned about what possible impact all the walking might have on my legs. Was I tiring them prior to the race?

Everything I read encouraged having "fresh legs" for a race; I was not going to have fresh legs; there was just too much to do, too much to enjoy.

As a runner, I have always refused to visually define the measurable distance, the actuality of how far I would be running in any race. This time was no different. I didn't want to dwell on the 26.2-mile race that I was there to accomplish. I wanted to enjoy my time with my family in the place we have always loved so much. I pushed any whispers of potential failure away and ignored any doubt that nudged my mind.

We walked together and covered the parks, had dining reservations, and visited the Walt Disney World® Marathon Weekend runDisney Health and Fitness Expo, where my son and

The Walt Disney World® Marathon Weekend runDisney Health and Fitness Expo

The author with her runner packet
(Photo taken by the author's daughter, Stephanie)

Disney characters © Disney

Official race autograph board at the Walt Disney World® Marathon Weekend
runDisney Health and Fitness Expo

I picked up our race numbers, runners' packets, and T-shirts, and where we also signed the official race autograph board. I love the energy of a race expo! The vibrations of anticipation and joy reverberate throughout, and this expo did just that. My son and I took pictures in front of our race banners, and we all mingled among the vendors and festivities, enjoying the excitement of the event.

"Dreams Come True" was my theme throughout the day, and at times, I had to remind myself it was exactly why I was there—to live my dream.

It was the mindset of the place where I chose to do it—the Walt Disney World Resort—that dreams do come true. I couldn't fail, it was impossible. The whispers of uncertainty waited patiently for my attention, but were dwarfed in such a place and found no home in my mind come race day.

The night before my race, I laid out my clothes and gear and surprisingly, had no problem falling asleep; I was definitely tired from the last few days of exploring the vast Resort complex. My alarm was set for 2:30am, yet I was awake and up just prior to it going off.

My first half-hour was spent meditating, praying, and giving thanks. I needed that time to center and stay present. I quietly moved around the room and systematically assembled myself, methodically going through my pre-race routine. I was tired, but wide awake and soaking in my morning. It was finally here and I wanted to stay in every moment.

By the end of today, I would be different. I knew that. When I initially selected this race and lovingly set it on my bucket list, I hadn't realized the emotional discard that would occur when I finally endured the path. I hadn't anticipated the monumental place it would represent in my life and the desperate need I would eventually have to reach my dream.

Years of anticipation were now assisting me in assembling the person who was to begin the race, overcoming the fears, disappointments and feelings I no longer had use for—baggage I had been carrying for years and was now eager to abandon along the path of 26.2 miles. I prepared my body and soul for the cleansing, the feat, and the accomplishment, the finality of a dream and the closure of a chapter in my life.

I had laid my necessary items out the night before and took my time placing each piece where it needed to be as if assembling a puzzle. I felt the fractured part of myself begin to come together, as if bonding as one was the only way I was reaching my goal. I could feel my soul pulling together memories and feelings I would like to forget, packing them as if they too were as important as my sport gels and music.

And so, I continued with my ritual; I chose running tights, but a short-sleeved shirt, since the weather promised to be beautifully warm by noon. My running shoes were securely laced with a pendant from my daughter reading: "26.2-courage to start, strength to endure, resolve to finish." It would be my physical reminder that my family loved me, believed in me, and supported my goal.

I had my throw-away sweatshirt and gloves for the morning stretch, my fanny pack containing sport gels, music, lip balm, inhaler, and my hat. I was almost complete. I turned and picked up my race number. It read #5610. I would be # 5610 today in a crowd of over 16,000. It also said my name—Mary—at the bottom and splashed across the top, it read MARATHON.

I was a marathon runner. The bib I was holding said so. All I had to do was pin it on and I was free to start with all the other athletes who assembled. I was free to challenge and push myself as far as I could; I had worked hard and earned the right to stand at the start and do my best.

Tears filled my eyes as I pinned the last fractured piece of me onto the band of my fanny pack. I turned and faced the mirror completed. I looked hard at the person who stood dressed in black with tears running down her cheeks. I was proud of myself and scared to death!

I knew what lay ahead—at least I thought I did. I knew the tribulations of 26.2 miles. I knew from my training that the distance was not going to be either swift or easy for me. And I knew my entire existence, at this moment, depended on completing it.

I knew the cleansing I was about to endure. I felt it awaiting my presence. I had sacrificed, struggled, and endured much and now I needed to carry with me the disappointments and setbacks and the hurts and pains from the past that had fractured the person I once was. I also need to carry the fears and doubts that existed in an old life, for which I no longer had use, so I could let it all go. I was at the precipice of my dream and I was going to embrace it with strength and confidence.

I was ready to be brave and set it free. I was ready to shed the negative, fear-based feelings and emotions along the race route in a continuous motion of cleansing.

Wiping my tears, I composed myself and gently walked past my sleeping son to awaken my best friend, who insisted on walking me to the hotel bus depot where I was to board my bus to Epcot and the race start. It was about 3:20am and I needed to be on a bus by 4am. We had some time to talk as we walked through the quiet, sleeping hallway down to the lobby.

I started to feel anxious and felt my pace quicken. My friend, keeping pace, reassured me I was prepared and ready. I needed to hear that at that moment, because feelings of fear and doubt were attempting to leak into my confidence.

The air was cold at the depot and we could see our breath. It was a crisp, dry morning and I was thankful for the sweatshirt and gloves I was wearing. Only minutes passed and my bus arrived. With a quick photo and good-bye hug, I boarded the warm, luxury bus and sat among the other runners. Yes, I was there, because I, too, was a runner.

I looked around at the others sitting around me, noticing their attire, water bottles, and various other necessities. I wondered why each was there. What was their motive to run, to awaken in the wee hours of the cold, dark morning to board a bus and then run 26.2 miles?

Sitting on the bus, watching others board, I felt a numbness start to fill me and I knew it was the shadow of the unknown. Something I learned about runners during my first distance event: they are a quiet, friendly bunch of people who love their sport and are happy to share their experiences when asked. They guard each other with mutual, nonjudgmental respect and realize each participant is there to challenge himself or herself, not compete with one another. Of course, the professional athletes are definitely competing; however, the runners who run for the enjoyment of the sport, who fill the other thousands of slots in an event, compete only against themselves, their personal records, and their dreams.

Resorting to my knowledge of runners and seeking relief of my pre-race uneasiness that summoned my attention, I turned to the person sitting next to me and began quizzing him on his intentions of the day.

He was quite friendly and shared that he had run both the half-marathon the day before and the full marathon for the last several years in a row. He said how he loved this race; it was his favorite and he looked forward to it every year. He lives locally and treats himself and his family to a weekend at the Walt World Resort for race weekend.

As we spoke, another person joined in and before long, my uneasiness passed and excitement took its place. Everyone had something to share and a reason, if just for sheer enjoyment, to be there. I knew my reason and I held it close to my heart, yet willingly shared it when I was asked *why*. It felt good to actually verbalize that running this marathon was my dream, a check-off on my bucket list. I knew I was in good company conversing, because we were all present in the moment and in a place where dreams coming true is expected.

We all spoke with a quiet, tired nervousness as we traveled to the starting area, all knowing the challenge of the run and the mystique of the marathon. We mutually respected one another for being there and were eager to share pointers and tips to ease the journey we were all about to take.

The bus drove us to the starting area, where a pre-race party was taking place. Once in the starting area, we all dispersed and new groups formed. A DJ was announcing, giving directions, and playing music. There were Walt Disney World Resort Characters and lines of runners waiting to have their picture taken with them. Tents had been set up for runners needing to check bags, which would be transported to the finish line for pick -up, and for any medical issues. Of course, there were rows upon rows of PortaPotties.

It was still dark and very cold, and I found it difficult to stay warm without moving around. Time passed quickly and the DJ signaled it was time to walk the long walk to the start corrals and urged everyone to begin moving. I was in corral D. In a race as large as the Walt Disney World® Marathon, runners are seeded and separated into groups according to their anticipated finish time, so everyone begins with the same start time as others of equal abilities.

We all began to move as directed, past even more portable toilets. As a runner, there never seems to be enough of the blue and green boxes. The crowd moved slowly, yet in a unified manner. It was hard for me to see where we were actually walking to due to my short height, although it was warm immersed in the crowd. We were packed together and being gently guided to our designated corrals.

En masse, we walked for at least 20 minutes or so, body to body, everyone following the person in front of them, navigating predestined roads and obeying the directions of security guards directing our path. Once at our morning destination, bright lights lit the way along make-shift corrals of temporary metal fencing that lined the actual starting area.

We would be called, one corral at a time, to start. Each corral would assemble at the starting point and given a firework send-off. The electronic chip placed in each runner's race bib would not begin counting until the runner crossed the start.

The crowd in Corral D was much more spread out and it felt more like a New Jersey morning than a Florida one. I waited in the cold, my breath quite visible and moved around to keep warm.

The DJ was now set up at the start of the race, along with a huge jumbo video screen, broadcasting and pumping up the runners. It was exciting and once again, I looked around at my fellow athletes to see what they were doing, wearing, and eating. From what I could tell, we were all cold. Some runners were dressed as Tinker Bell or Peter Pan. Some wore Mickey Mouse ears, others tutus. But for the most part, we were all dressed to run. Tights, sweatshirts, gloves, hats, and choice of music seemed to be the norm.

My daughter had encouraged me to dress up for the race, but 26.2 miles is a long way in a tutu. I know myself, and I become so uncomfortable in my own skin after a long run, and with the frequency of potty breaks, a tutu would become a nuisance. So, I had declined and was glad I had as I waited for my corral to be called.

I was excited, nervous, and scared. My mind started to step in and comfort me as I felt my nerves awaken. "Just a long run this morning, just like at home," I told myself. " I'm only out for a long run. I'm packed and ready and after a couple of hours, I will be done. Then I can get back to my family and having fun."

Around us, corrals were being organized, one by one. While I waited, I decided to focus inward and meditate and feel the moment and enjoy my time in a place I would experience only once. I breathed, in and then out, finding my center. I was standing at the very start of my long-awaited race, wanted to experience being present and log this momentous moment into my long-term memory. I was finally here! I had made it this far, one year in the making, 16 years in my heart and I was going to soon put one foot in front of the other and live my dream!!

Then it started—the playing of the national anthem. I had never participated in a sport before I began running as an adult, so to stand and hear the *Star-Spangled Banner* played before an event in which I was participating was quite emotional. As a child, I had been taught how to stand still and respect our nation's hymn, so to have it played before *MY* event brings tears to my eyes and a lump in my throat. I am proud to stand tall and free, and the initiation of the playing truly makes me feel like an athlete. I was standing, in MY country, and MY National Anthem was playing. I offered a prayer of gratitude as I stood

Start of the Walt Disney World® Marathon with fireworks
(Photo courtesy of Disney Photos, © Disney.)

proud and wiped the tears from my eyes with my gloved hands, knowing the event was about to begin.

It was time, approximately 5:30am. The initial start commenced and fireworks exploded as the wheelchair and premium runners began. Soon after that, in synchronicity, each corral was called in order and released to run.

I was ready. I was also cold, scared, and exhilarated. I kept my thoughts centered to remain present and stretched in place just prior to my corral's request to line up. We all packed into the starting area and the energy around me illuminated as brightly as the fireworks being lit. With a bang, we were off!

Waving to the camera, seeing ourselves on the jumbo television, I promised myself to enjoy my day and my quest and soak in all that was around me. I waved, I ran, and I breathed. I found my rhythm quickly and waved to the crowd of people cheering us on along the side of the road in the dark morning hours. People I didn't even know lined the highway to catch a glimpse of their runner and to cheer all of us on.

I settled into my rhythm and it felt good. I was running MY race today. I was not running against the clock, or to prove anything or even set a PR, a personal record. I was there to be in the moment that presented itself, one step at a time. I was much slower than I had been fifteen years ago, yet in my mind's eye, I had learned that I am slower because I am taking my time to be present and experience the moment at hand. Today, that was my very intention.

I had grown past the insecurities of racing and running, of having short legs and being overweight. I was here to live and enjoy my time in the flow of the marathon and make myself emotionally available for the enjoyment of the experience and the cleansing that takes place.

I was ready to endure and expand into the very fabric of the mystique and find myself at the finish a different, more confident, stronger person than I started. So I would take my time, run my race, and look around at all magic. I would focus on my goal, believe in myself. I am shedding the unwanted, unnecessary, and outdated pieces of myself and gathering along the way the courage, faith, and tenacity I needed to complete my goal.

The runners began to spread out and I ran, paying attention to my foot strike and the angle of the road surface. I was aware of the ghosts of my past related to running on an uneven ground.

Around mile 3, I had warmed up and was ready to take off my gloves and sweatshirt. There were other clothes along the roadside, so as I removed my clothes, I also viewed this activity as symbolically shedding my emotional baggage. I intentionally folded my sweatshirt, made sure my gloves stayed together as a pair, and placed them on the grass at the side of the road we were running on. Then I let the gloves and sweatshirt go, tucking within them the pieces of me I no longer needed. I smiled at the symbolic nature of the release, turned, and continued to put one foot in front of the other. I was letting go, I could feel the beginning of the cleansing, the releasing, and the freedom.

The race route turned and took us into Epcot. We ran as a tighter pack through the monorail turnstiles and under Spaceship Earth; we continued into the entrance of World Showcase, where someone shouted, "Pictures!"

Photographers lined the entrance way into the beautifully lit, sparkling World Showcase. All the buildings were illuminated with twinkling white lights; enormous, fierce torches roared and blazed, reflecting off the smooth surface of the lagoon. The energy that pulsed lifted me up as if I were floating; I felt my body easily gliding through the wave of adrenaline. It was a magnificent and breathtaking sight!

As I ran, I enjoyed the magical distractions and walked faithfully through the water stations. I high-fived the band members playing alongside the road and thanked them for being there to cheer us on. I waved at the characters who accumulated lines for pictures, but I couldn't stop. I hadn't brought a camera, a conscious choice. I knew I had to keep moving and stay with my rhythm.

The sun rose bright and the day promised to be warm and quite beautiful. I was running towards the Magic Kingdom and looking forward to finally running through Cinderella Castle. I ran past the 10-mile marker and completed a physical check. Truthfully, I was feeling a little tired and stiff. I stopped to stretch and silently, with intent, sent love and light to my legs.

I breathed and began running towards the confirmation of my dream. I was so excited to be present in the moment; I completed the intentional breathing and kept my eyes wide, eagerly seeking the cherished landmark.

The uniqueness of the Walt Disney World® Marathon is that while running, the landmarks are not clearly visible, then all of a sudden, they appear on a turn of the path. I looked for the castle, knew I was close. I couldn't see it, but I could hear the cheers of the spectators along Main Street, U.S.A.

I continued as directed and cast members now lined the route, cheering and clapping, offering smiles and words of encouragement. They also confidently reassured the runners that the Magic Kingdom was only a few steps away.

My kids always said we weren't really at the Walt Disney World Resort until we arrived at the Magic Kingdom. The memory of their voices echoed, I felt my heart leap and a lump formed in my throat as I ran alongside Tony's Restaurant, where we had eaten the night before and celebrated my pending birthday. I ran into the cheers of the crowds awaiting the runners. The energy was invigorating and I felt electrified!

As I made the right turn onto Main Street, U.S.A., I eagerly looked up to see the confirmation of my presence, the validation that I WAS at the Walt Disney World Resort and the most beautiful castle, Cinderella Castle! The vision seized my heart. I gasped and realized in that instant that I WAS living my dream. I WAS really here, in the present moment, running, moving toward the enormous structure that symbolically signified my dream. My eyes blurred and felt tears begin to course down my cheeks. "You can't run and cry at the same time," I told myself.

Cinderella Castle and crowds of onlookers.

Struggling to regain my composure, I embraced the magic and energy of Main Street, U.S.A.

So many people lined the race route and cheered, shouting words of encouragement and admiration. Music played and horns blew. I ran, feeling my heart beating with excitement and carrying me to the place I longed to be. One of the few benefits to being a slower runner, is that there is more space in which to run. Thus, as I rounded the path through Fantasyland, to the back of the castle, past the Tea Cups, I was not competing for space. I slowed, feeling stiffness creep in, but nevertheless, enjoying the moment. I let it engulf me whole, carrying me gently as I turned and entered the rear castle gate.

I felt the coolness of the shaded corridor brush my face as I ran my fingers along the mosaic tiles that lined the walls. I allowed myself to FEEL—the coolness of the air, the roughness of the tile, the hardness of the ground, the pounding of my heart, the lump once again welling up in my throat, the soft tears in my eyes. I relished the presence of my fellow runners sharing my sacred space, visualizing the bright sunshine at the tunnel's end. I was present in the moment, all senses alive and in tune. I could feel the energy flowing around me, through me, like a delicate cloud caressing my body, carrying me through the tall passageway to the other side.

Running through Cinderella Castle, which I saw as a physical metaphor for this entire race, I willingly entered the shadow of the hallway, running my fingers over the mosaics, the pieces of my life, only then to emerge anew, leaving the old and the past behind, and bursting into the light, a new life, continuing on my path. I longed to live in the moment, to be present in life. I was finally cleansing and letting go of what was no longer needed. There, I left pieces of myself as I continued on into the warmth of the sunlight of my new life.

A field of photographers, runners, cast members and spectators awaited me as I emerged from Cinderella Castle. They were smiling, cheering, and also immersed in the joy of the moment. I knew no one had known the transformation I had just experienced; I couldn't help but feel the Universe was there to applaud my achievement. I waved in acknowledged gratitude as I wiped the last tear from my eyes and turned toward Liberty Square, proceeding through Frontierland and running out of the Magic Kingdom.

HALF-WAY

My legs were beginning to stiffen and I again stopped for a thorough stretch. I was drinking at each water station and eating as well. My performance time was slower than I had hoped and I could feel myself slowing more. The emotional shift I had just experienced left me slightly drained, but amazingly lighter.

I was approaching the 13.1 mile mark, where those participating in the relay would be meeting their partners. I couldn't help but wish my race was finishing as well, while acknowledging that I was only half the way done.

The road from Magic Kingdom to Disney's Animal Kingdom is a long, flat, straight run and the warmth of the day was growing. The sun shone brightly and my fellow racers and I couldn't help to comment on the beauty of the day.

My body, however, was feeling the strain. My left leg, with its old ITB injury, was beginning to nag at me relentlessly, burning along my entire left leg. I decided to walk a brisk walk, knowing the body uses different muscles to walk than run. I chose to give my ITB a rest. I would walk the next couple of miles, stretch, and then run a few more.

My right knee was feeling fine, so I had hoped the respite and switching to other leg muscles would allow my ITB to be forgiving and choose to participate again without complaint. I walked an easy, fast three miles and continued to grab fluids at each stop offered. I ate the gels and my strength was steady and strong.

There were characters and cast members along the way and the peacefulness of the roadway caused me to enjoy my surroundings and the company of others, rather than resorting to my headphones.

I kept a good walk pace, but when I attempted a run, I was immediately stricken with a sharp pain in my left leg. It felt twisted and stiff and burned like fire; the stretching was unsuccessful. I was faced with a crossroad I had not anticipated. I had not anticipated that my LEFT leg would protest; it was not in the plan. I had been faithful to my stretching, my physical therapy, my rest days; I had eaten appropriately and lost the extra weight to relieve my joints, yet it would be my ITB that would not cooperate.

Nevertheless, I kept walking briskly and that felt good. I was not physically stressed and my legs otherwise didn't hurt; I would keep to my pace until I could figure out a plan. Maybe I needed to just rest it from running a few more miles, and then I could run in the last five strong. I walked. My time was steady, but much slower than I had anticipated during training and I started to emotionally feel the length of the 26.2 miles.

It was a long, stretch of roadway. Miraculously, I found myself in Disney's Animal Kingdom. I had begun to feel the daze of the run, the humming related to the continuous motion of my body, and the physical demands had started to supersede my emotional determination. I relished the luxury of a real lavatory and soap and water to wash my hands and wipe my face. I could feel the persistent aching and stiffness throughout my battered body and I longed to continue on so that I could be finished.

The stony pathways in Disney's Animal Kingdom were narrow and my swollen feet felt every uneven surface. The theme park was open to guests and it seemed that as quickly as we ran into Disney's Animal Kingdom, we ran out and back onto the roadway.

I knew my family was waiting for me; they were getting regular updates via text messages thanks to the computer chip in my race bib, and I was relieved. I was moving at a much slower pace than I had anticipated. Knowing they knew where I was on the race route gave me peace. I wanted to be finished; I was tired of struggling, tired of moving and pushing myself. I wanted to see their faces and put the marathon behind me. I was becoming discouraged; the walking made the distance longer and my mindset shifted. I found myself desperate to enjoy the experience and stay focused.

It was getting hotter and more humid, and it felt as though the end of the race had stretched and was much farther away than it had been when I started. It was like a dream, when the door at the end of the hallway is visible, but keeps moving farther and farther away, creating the illusion it can never be reached.

In the hot Florida sun, I was really sweating, drenched through and the occasional, yet minimal, warm breeze was welcomed. With both legs tight and protesting, my body becoming fatigued, the finish line felt unreachable. I was pushing myself with each step, attempting to maintain some sort of rhythm, some sort of flow. But instead, each deliberate step was a painful, desperate challenge.

My feet ached and I could feel them burning in my shoes. The pavement was hot and the sweltering heat affected my every move. I felt thirsty, but my stomach felt as if it wanted no parts of anything, food or drink. But I knew deep down that I had to keep pressing on, keep pushing myself. I forced myself to focus and visualize myself crossing the finish line. I kept telling myself that if I just run now, I'll never have to run again.

Soon, I was back on the highway, not even sure what mile marker I had passed. No shade, no breeze, no Disney's Hollywood Studios in sight. I was aimlessly following the crowd, the signs, straining to hear or see any sign of the next theme park.

Tired and stiff, I felt every bit my age. I continued to walk as fast as I could, attempting to maintain some kind of a pace, wanting it to end as quickly as possible. I have to say I was disappointed in myself, after all this time, embarrassed to even think that as I approached mile 20, I was ready to quit—not just from exhaustion or dehydration, but from the illusion of never finishing.

In those moments, I really contemplated just stopping and ending the challenge. It was a conscious thought I considered with every step; I was tired of struggling, tired of not being able to run and forced to walk, which hadn't been in the training plan at all, but somehow, it was my only chance of finishing.

Tears of desperation filled my eyes and the empty pit in my stomach grew. I had trained for one entire year, rearranged my whole life, dreamed of accomplishing this goal for years, and here I was, entertaining the idea of quitting. I really did; it was a genuinely well-thought-out concept, one I couldn't believe would have ever surfaced.

I was tired of the fight, tired of the moving. I hurt, ached, needed another bathroom, and just wanted it all to be over. The miles seemed so much longer now and I was moving so much slower, steady and strong, but slower.

What would I say to my family waiting for me if I chose to quit? How would I even live with myself after quitting on my dream? The nausea of the thoughts I was entertaining churned in my gut. Then my soul whispered, "Pain is temporary; quitting is forever. This moment, this chance, will never come again, and you've already come this far." I decided that all I really had to do for the moment was put one foot in front of the other—and so I did.

In the fog of the run, I started to motivate myself into completing the distance ahead. *One mile until the wall... I can do that; I can do one more mile. Then after that, I only have five to go. Three to Disney's Hollywood Studios, two through Epcot, then 0.2 to finish. I can walk five miles fast, maybe even run the last two.* I counted the miles ahead. I breathed love and light into my tired, aching, fatigued body, which was now significantly feeling the Florida heat and the hours on the road.

Keep drinking, I told myself. *Drink and eat through the wall.*

The bridge over the highway toward mile 21 slowed almost all the runners in my immediate pack. It was so hot, the incline challenged my tired physique, and this, I felt, was the infamous "wall" marathoners hit, which is when things transition from being pretty hard to being really, really hard. It is the point at which mind and body are simultaneously challenged. I still wanted to quit; I really did. I couldn't believe the thought continued to sweep through my mind, but it did, testing my strength and my will and promising a haunting whisper of relief to my agony.

An argument ensued within me, battling the need to end the suffering and the need to be finished. *This was madness!* I couldn't even remember why this race was so important for me; I was trying to rationalize my decision as I continued to place one sore foot in front of the other. I couldn't remember—all I knew is that I was doing it, it was taking so much longer than I thought it would, I was exhausted, achy, hot, and my mind was a blur. I wanted to be done, and no finish line was in site. Not even an entire theme park could be seen! *Where was I?*

"Mile 21" read the marker and in my futile attempt to eat a banana and drink an energy drink from a food station, I glanced at my shoe. There was the pendant my daughter had given me threaded through my laces. It was there, reflecting the sunlight, pulling me back into reality. My family was waiting for me, and yes, I had to finish—for them and for me. I couldn't clearly rationalize why I was where I was, but I knew I had to keep moving as quickly as I could and complete this task I had given up so much of my life to do. I knew I couldn't quit.

I wish I could say I enjoyed the final stretch of my race, but the last 5.2 miles were indescribably challenging. I was only able to do a brisk walk. My legs were stiff and my ITB burned and was knotted even tighter. My feet felt like marshmallows, and I was anxious to have it all be over. A mild fear that I might not ever finish coursed through me, and hope seemed far away. Then my soul whispered, "Behind the fear is the person you want to be. Keep moving!" I was disappointed in myself for the doubts and wishes for the race to be over. I so wanted to stay focused in the moment and enjoy the day.

After all, I had given up so much of myself this past year to participate and complete this endeavor and it truly was almost over. I could hear music coming from behind the trees, signaling I was close to Disney's Hollywood Studios.

Only about 4 miles to go. I can do 4 miles. I am a distance runner. So I stepped it up, the best I could.

I refocused and relished the sites of the park. I kept walking at a steady clip and finally believed the finish at Epcot actually existed. The race route continued through Disney's Hollywood Studios, through the crowds, not really cheering now, but waiting to cross over the race route, directed by cast members.

The parks had opened to the public and even though the Walt Disney World Resort cast members were pleasant, smiling, and gave us the upmost respect while yielding the right-of-way, those enjoying their vacations had to wait for runners to pass before they could cross the race route to their next destination—a humbling experience for the distance runners.

The cheers of the crowds along the race route had transformed into impatience with a hint of annoyance. I could understand their stance. However, I was struggling through the last few miles of a race that I too had wished was long over.

I had begun my quest with no intention of being on the course for as long as I had been. It was taking everything in my being to pull myself through the last several miles.

Please be patient with me, I thought as I passed the visitors, doing my best to quicken my step.

Once through Disney's Hollywood Studios, I turned onto the waterway path between Epcot and Disney's Hollywood Studios, where I was greeted with a welcome, light, cool breeze and shaded areas on my way back into Epcot. It felt so refreshing and it lifted my spirits to keep going. I only had 2.2 miles to go until the finish. Eagerly, I sought to see the finish line marker, Spaceship Earth.

I knew I would be seeing my family soon; they promised to be along the route and with the text updates they were receiving, they would be able to predict my location. My feet were so sore, my body so tired. However; as long as I didn't run, I wasn't in any real pain, and the purpose of my endeavor cleared in my mind's eye.

I was almost done! I was beginning to refocus and realize that my willfulness to quit was actually the final stage of the cleansing. It was now almost complete. I couldn't see it in the moment; distress and disbelief clouded my vision as I had to endure the emotions lying at the very bottom of my soul, unearthed by the marathon mystique rising up through me and being released. The weaknesses and self-doubt that had festered were being flushed out, leaving behind a new openness for self-healing and growth.

Calmness flowed through me with the presence of the realization and the cool breeze remained and with a little more than two miles to go, I knew I would finish.

Entering Epcot through the International Gateway, once again I turned into cheering crowds. The race route yielded right to run around World Showcase; Spaceship Earth was off to my left in the distance, marking my completion.

I felt excited and could feel the final unwanted weights of my past life dropping from me, crashing to the ground, as if the chains binding them to me were disintegrating with every step. I cannot explain why at this time in my event this occurred; I have always loved the beauty of strolling through the countries of World Showcase, relaxing during an otherwise busy vacation. However, the time I was now spending in one of my favorite spots, was instead removing whatever remained of the insecurities, fears, and doubts I was ready to release and let go.

Perhaps this was a comfort zone with a promise of completion or a familiar place with loving memories open to receive the remains of a life left behind. Whatever the reason, the atmosphere that reigned over my final miles was exhilarating and energized. I kept moving toward my goal, desperate to run the last mile. I attempted my running stride, but my left leg screamed in protest. The twisted and stiff appendage was not going to cooperate. So, I continued walking, now at a feverish clip, toward my journey's end, looking for my family. I wanted to finish strong. I had trained and practiced; I wanted to come in looking like the runner I was inside. Instead, I walked, my head held high, keeping pace.

Turning out of World Showcase into Future World and toward the finish line is where I saw my family sitting precisely

The author running the last mile, waving to her family.

at the 0.2 mark of 26.2 miles. I have to confess, they saw me first, calling to me and cheering.

My daughter held a sign: "I'm a complete stranger and I am proud of you." My best friend waved her sign: "Your Magical Dream Has Come True!" They were all cheering, reassuring and encouraging the runners. "You're almost there, just a little more!" as they patiently waited for me. Once again, I felt tears well in my eyes and a wave of relief flow through me as I turned toward them and waved.

My daughter, having achieved the coveted runDisney Coast-to-Coast Race Challenge medal the previous year; my son, who had finished his first half-marathon, the Walt Disney World Half-Marathon the day before; and my best friend, who had run her

My daughter's "complete stranger" sign.
Disney characters © Disney.

first and last 10K with me several years ago, all sat in support of my fellow runners and awaited my arrival.

The two young women running together alongside me actually cried as they read their signs, which validated the great feat we were accomplishing. We were almost done and relieved at the reassurance. Pride filled me at that moment—not for myself, but for the loving intention, support, and encouragement my family was giving to me and to others. They loudly shouted out the names of the runners, reading their names on their race bibs and cheered on the exhausted athletes, encouraging them to keep going.

Yes, they were waiting for me, but were also sharing their love and respect for the other athletes who passed by, sending them kindness and support for a job well done. Their signs and encouragement filled me with feelings of pride and unconditional love. I was so thankful I had not given up along the way. I waved, smiled and so happy to see them. I posed for a picture and then turned away to complete my quest, wiping the tears from my eyes as I followed the last few bends into the finishing area.

Finally, I could see the finish line! It was an enormous area, bold and strong, just waiting for me to arrive. Photographers lined the sides of the roadway. The announcers called random runner names and hometowns. Music played and spectators cheered.

I attempted to run, but my legs were so tight and twisted. I had wanted to run the last stretch despite my pain. I wanted to finish running.

The Walt Disney World® Marathon finish line (Disney characters © Disney)

So, with every last ounce of strength and endurance, I ran my last 0.1 over the finish line, stepping firmly on the time clock mat and raising my arms in power with happiness, fulfillment, and complete joy.

Running across the Walt Disney World® Marathon finish line
(Photo courtesy of Disney Photos, © Disney).

I had lived so much of my life yearning for this exact moment. I had given up so much of the past year to be able to cross the Walt Disney World® Marathon finish line and close this chapter of my life. I held onto every thought, every feeling, and everything happening around me. I had practiced living in the moment—for this moment—to remember it and place it lovingly in my heart. I was now able to check the space on my bucket list, *DONE*, forever and grow as a person and as a soul from the experience.

I could feel the fractured pieces that had been delicately laid for me in Sedona meld together as I transitioned into the person I was meant to be. I had completed the cleansing and expelled all the feelings that no longer served me. I had let go of the phantoms and chains that had weighed me down and overcome the self-doubt and insecurities. I had survived the challenge of crossing the Walt Disney World® Marathon finish line, where I found that I was eagerly waiting for myself to arrive. We came together—the once damaged, insecure, anxious human and the confident higher self—finding each other, embracing with light and love.

COMPLETION

O nce across the Walt Disney World® Marathon finish line, runners were immediately greeted by cast members holding their medals. I felt tears of joy well up as my own medal was placed around my neck. My long-awaited trophy now hung next to my heart, where in my heart space, it belonged.

On January 8, 2012, I completed the Walt Disney World (R) Marathon
in 6:43:25—6 hours, 43 minutes, and 25 seconds.
Disney characters © Disney

A "Medal with Mouse Ears" was now mine, shiny gold and beautiful!! It was a surreal feeling, almost like the birth of a child. I kept looking at it, finding it so hard to believe it was really mine. Yet, there it was in my hands, around my neck, belonging to me. Joy, unexplainable joy, flooded over me in that instant. I succumbed to the emotion, tucking it all safely in my heart.

I posed for my finalist picture after crossing the finish line in 6 hours, 43 minutes and 25 seconds, over two hours past my projected time. Taking small sips of water from a cup, I walked

Joe and Mary with finisher medals, Stephanie in her crown
Disney characters © Disney

slowly into the finishing corral to wait for my family. We had a predetermined area selected after having met my son the day before.

I ached, was stiff and sweat-drenched, and was glad I could finally slow down and rest. The ground looked hard and so far away to even begin to attempt to sit down, but I did so anyway, then snacking and drinking. I spent the brief time in a quiet prayer of thanks for the inner strength and the ability to endure.

I crossed the finish line hours past my expected time and was tired beyond explanation. With cheers, hugs, and accolades, my family found my sore, tired body on the ground. I confessed to them that I had wanted to quit, that I couldn't even believe I entertained the thought, but that I did. I told them of my experience and struggle and how excited I was to see them on the route. They all said I didn't even look tired, but more like a weight had been lifted. I felt that. The heavy emotional weight that I'd been carrying was actually visible to others, and now had been lifted. I felt lighter. I felt the communing of my soul and spirit dwelling within my body as if new spaces and a new openness existed within me.

I had done it! I was proud of myself, really proud. I struggled through the physically and emotional rollercoaster of the marathon and came through a new person, a whole person, someone who had pushed herself to the very limit she could and survived. I was in that moment, the best I could be.

Daughter Stephanie getting ready to cheer me on.

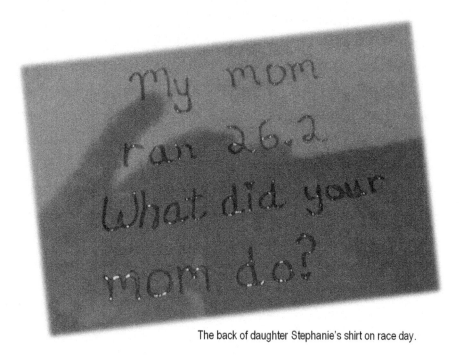

The back of daughter Stephanie's shirt on race day.

Joe & Mary, proud finishers.
Disney characters © Disney

My medal with mouse ears.
(Photo courtesy of Disney Photos, © Disney)

Relief and gratitude flooded me. I was so thankful it was over. My family and I boarded a bus back to the hotel and I was eager to share my experiences, as they were.

It felt so good to finally sit down and just rest. I could feel my body and my mind now relaxing and quieting and succumbing to the moment of completion. My family was there to guide me through the transition. They had had to check out prior to my finishing the race, since I was on the course for so long, but the hotel held our luggage and we were free to continue to use the facilities until midnight. So I was able to shower and dress in the fitness center. Afterwards, my family and I relaxed on the soft sofas in the hotel lobby—where a surprise awaited me.

Delirious, weak, and stiff, I sat as instructed and awaited their contribution to the gathering. Suddenly, my daughter pulled from a bag a beautiful package, consisting of a plaque, a bronze medal and a case, sprinkled with shiny glitter, arranged on a stunning silver platter, wrapped in crystal-clear cellophane, and adorned with the most beautiful bow. I was simply at a loss for words.

Mickey Mouse © Disney

Let it be known to all who view this medal that

Mary Townsend

Is officially honored as part of a Disney tradition that includes all
the dreamers and doers who have gone before.
Your character, courage and hope as seen in

going for your dream.

Allows us to honor you with a Disney Magical Triumph!
May you carry this medal with pride and be an example
of dreams-come-true to all who cross your path.

This recognition and medal proclaim your rights
to never lose sight of your dreams,
the freedom to follow your heart and the honor of receiving a
Disney Magical Triumph!

Mickey Mouse - CEO
Chief Ear Officer

The plaque and medal (opposite) given to me by my family.
Tinker Bell © Disney

The plaque read:

Let it be known to all who view this medal that
Mary Townsend
Is officially honored as part of a Disney Tradition that includes all
the dreamers and doers who have gone before.
Your character, courage and hope as seen in
Going for your dream
Allows us to honor you with a Disney Magical Triumph!
May you carry this medal with pride and be an example
Of dreams-come-true to all who cross your path

This recognition and medal proclaim your rights
To never lose sight of your dreams,
the freedom to follow your heart and the honor of receiving a
Disney Magical Triumph!

Signed: Mickey Mouse
Chief Ear Officer

I was speechless and of course, I cried.

Together, we enjoyed our last afternoon at the Walt Disney World Resort, sitting outside by the water, eating pizza, recapping our experiences. The breezes blew as we shared our different experiences, how each of us had been touched by others throughout race weekend.

All of us had changed; we had grown in appreciation of each other and of ourselves. We had created new memories, joys, and accomplishments that will last our lifetimes. Then we said our farewell to the Walt Disney World Resort, and all of us tiredly boarded Disney's Magical Express to take us to the airport.

GROWTH

Completing my marathon and feeling the weight of MY Medal with Mouse Ears around my neck, solidified my quest toward my dream and provided me with a physical representation that I was able to pick up and hold with my heart.

Lovingly, I could now place the years of discontent into an imaginary box, the pain and fears having been cleansed away. My old self followed suit and I sealed it with peaceful finality. I had crossed the finish line of my race and left behind the person I used to be. I had completed the 26.2 miles, releasing and shedding the fears, unhappiness, anxiety, and insecurities. I had pushed through the walls I had built and emerged the person I had been all along. My soul had found its way out by shattering the shell that had encompassed me and releasing the light that passionately desired to shine brightly.

I had crossed the finish line and my transformation was complete. The struggles and sacrifices of the previous twelve months, and 26.2 miles, were gone as I raised my arms up and crossed the finish line into my new life. I was ready now, having cleared the last of the cobwebs left from an old life; I was ready to emerge anew.

Through my Walt Disney World® Marathon experience, I learned of many things that were rooted deep within my being and that only now am I able to see and share their existence.

I learned I am human—very basic, but nevertheless, a mindset in which one must choose to forgive oneself of decisions past. All things happen for a reason and in this moment, I am where I am supposed to be.

I learned to be thankful and that I am so blessed to be able to feel the love and light in my life completely, now that my shell has been broken and removed.

I learned that I am strong, determined, and disciplined and when pushed to the limit, I can succeed and push through.

I learned that 26.2 miles is a very far distance and because I chose to run it, I was faced with an endurance event that broke me down, cleansed me emotionally, physically, and spiritually, to reveal the light that abides deep within me.

I learned that what I had been searching for all along was love. Not only self-love or sharing love, but to feel love through-out my entire being. Love is the universal life force and even though it resides at the very core of everything, I was having a hard time finding it. I couldn't feel it though the sadness, stress, and anxiety; its energy was being blocked by illusions, fears, and situations that made me feel trapped and lost.

I learned that love truly connects us all and the shared experience of life provides the classroom in which to learn, grow, and enjoy even the most intimate of dreams. The loving support and encouragement of others, especially family, motivates and lifts the heart and its desire to fulfill its quest, then expands to share its victory in celebration. It is life at its best and love at its purest; it is the light of the collective soul.

I learned to trust myself, my instincts, my decisions, and my inner voice.

I learned that behind my fears and doubts dwells the person I want to be.

I found peace and solace in my meditation, my running, and eventually my life.

And I found that the person I am deep within was waiting for me to find her all along, as she stood on the finish line at the end of a marathon, ready to embrace me and welcome me home.

I learned that no matter the wish or desire, as long as love and the conviction of my dreams come from my heart, I am invincible.

About the Author

Years have passed and my medal with mouse ears hangs where I see it every day.

It still remains the most powerful reminder of how important it is to be brave when pursuing my heart's innermost desires, and how important it is to love one's self enough to grow and change, no matter how difficult.

I no longer run. Crossing the finish line at the Walt Disney World® Marathon was the last time I was able to stride. I continue to keep active and eat healthy.

I continue to practice a holistic view of wellness and of life, which reminds us that the mind, body, and spirit are all interconnected.

My Reiki practice is a daily commitment and the cornerstone of my belief that we are all connected in life, with light, by love.

I wish you much joy, peace, and happiness as you pursue the dreams of your heart.

Love and light,
Mary

I can be reached on Facebook: facebook.com/Onelightwellness
By email: onelightwellness@gmail.com
And via my website: Onelightwellness.wix.com/onelightwellness